Exploring Informational Texts

Exploring Informational Texts

FROM THEORY TO PRACTICE

Linda Hoyt

Margaret Mooney

Brenda Parkes

Editors

Heinemann

Portsmouth, NH

Heinemann

361 Hanover Street
Portsmouth, NH 03801–3912
www.heinemann.com

Offices and agents throughout the world

The editors and publisher wish to thank those who have generously given permission to
reprint borrowed material:
Figure 9-1: Material from *Spiders* is reprinted by permission of Newbridge Educational
Publishing. Copyright by Newbridge Educational Publishing, New York, a Haights Cross
Communications Company.
Figure 9-2: Material from *Our Journey West* is reprinted by permission of the National
Geographic Society. Copyright by the National Geographic Society.
Figure 10-2: Material from *Big Dig* is reprinted by permission of Newbridge Educational
Publishing. Copyright by Newbridge Educational Publishing, New York, a Haights Cross
Communications Company.

Credits Continue on p. 188.

Library of Congress Cataloging-in-Publication Data
    Exploring informational texts : from theory to practice / Linda Hoyt, Margaret
Mooney, Brenda Parkes, editors.
        p.   cm.
    Includes bibliographical references and index.
    ISBN 0-325-00472-2
    1. Language arts (Elementary).   2. Exposition (Rhetoric)—Study and teaching
(Elementary).   I. Hoyt, Linda.   II. Mooney, Margaret E.   III. Parkes, Brenda.
    LB1576 .E98 2003
    372.6–dc21   2002154317

Editor: Lois Bridges
Production: Patricia Adams
Production coordination: Abigail M. Heim
Typesetter: TechBooks
Cover coordination: Renée Le Verrier
Cover design: Catherine Hawkes, Cat and Mouse
Cover Image: © Image 100, "Educating Children"/Wonderfile
Manufacturing: Steve Bernier

Printed in the United States of America on acid-free paper
10 09 08   VP   7 8 9 10

Contents

Note to the Reader

There are many voices and opinions in this book, and that is as it should be! As more teachers become familiar with the nuances of guided reading and comfortable using informational texts as a vehicle for instruction from the emergent stage of reading development, our journey toward understanding and competence matches that of a class of students on their reading journey. This book does not claim to be either definitive or exclusive in its exploration of informational texts. The contributors have chosen to share aspects of their current understanding to create a montage of ideas and suggestions. Our common goal is to make informational texts accessible and enjoyable. The book also includes reflections from authors of informational texts for young readers. These reflections are offered in the hope that they will encourage more teachers to pick up the pen and write informational texts, for unless you have walked the path you expect students to take, it is hard to be a truly effective guide.

Although the book works as a whole, please dip and delve through the parts to create your own sequence. This will give you a chance to create your own understandings as you mix and match the different voices in the essays. After all, the reading of informational texts is not so much about gathering information, as it is about selecting and using information.

We invite you to wonder, to question, and to join hands with your students in *Exploring Informational Texts*!

Celebrating Informational Text

Guided reading and writing with informational texts enables children to learn about the world while learning to read, and ensures that explicit instruction in reading strategies and writer's craft continues throughout the grades.

Emergent readers reading, wondering, and growing as readers.

Explorations of text features such as the index and table of contents support learners of all developmental phases as they build knowledge about the world.

Guided reading with informational texts provides time for explicit teaching, activation of prior knowledge, and direct instruction in the strategies readers use to make meaning.

Small-group and individual conferences lay a foundation for growth in reading and writing of informational texts.

Photographs by Kathy Baird, Staff Developer and Reading Recovery Teacher/leader, McMinnville, Oregon.

PART 1

Bringing Informational Texts into Focus

Informational texts comprise the majority of reading and writing done by adults and represent the majority of passages offered to students in standardized tests. Informational literacy must be seen with new eyes, and every teacher from kindergarten through university has an opportunity to make a difference. As reflective practitioners, this is an exciting time to look closely at the texts we offer our students, consider balance between fiction and informational texts, and to wonder in harmony about our next steps.

The chapters in this section deal with the vital importance of rethinking the role informational texts play in daily instruction and the transformations in teacher thinking that accompany the shift.

1

Informational Text?
The Research Says,
"Yes!"

NELL K. DUKE

3.6 minutes per day . . . in a study I conducted in first-grade class-rooms, that was the average amount of time spent with informa-tional text! And for classrooms in low socioeconomic status (SES) districts, the average was only 1.4 minutes per day! (Duke 2000). This and other studies suggest that informational text is scarce in

American elementary schools, especially in the primary grades. This has not always been true, but it has been true for much of the history of American schooling.

Should this be so? Are there good reasons not to include informational text in early schooling? Two reasons often cited for excluding informational text from early schooling are that young children cannot really handle informational text and that young children do not like informational text. In a review of literature in this area, we found that neither of these reasons has a good basis in research. Research indicates that young children can be successful with informational text if given the opportunity. Studies show that even young children can learn content from informational text, can understand and retell informational texts, can learn about the language and features of informational text, can respond to and discuss informational text, and can even write informational text! Moreover, some young children actually prefer informational text and are most interested in topics commonly addressed through informational forms. (See Dreher 2000; Duke, Bennett-Armistead, and Roberts 2002; and Duke 2002 for reviews.)

But just because young children can do all this, should they? Are there good reasons to include informational text in elementary school, and even in primary-grade classrooms? Research suggests that there are:

Six Serious Reasons to Include Informational Text

1. **Informational text is key to success in later schooling.** We have all heard that from around fourth grade on "reading to learn" is a big focus in school (Chall 1983). Children encounter more and more textbooks and other informational texts as they move through the grades. The tests students take contain increasingly more difficult informational texts. College curricula are replete with informational reading of a variety of types. Perhaps if we include more informational text in early schooling we will put children in a better position to handle the reading and writing demands of later schooling. We would like to see a day when children "read to learn" and, for that matter,

"learn to read," from the earliest days of schooling and throughout their school careers.

2. **Informational text is ubiquitous in the larger society.** Several studies have looked at what kinds of things people write *outside of* schooling—what adults read and write in their workplaces, homes, and communities. Again and again, these studies have shown that adults read a great deal of nonfiction, including informational text (e.g., Venezky 1982; Smith 2000). This is not likely to change, and in fact, in our increasingly information-based economy it may only increase. A statistic that I find quite remarkable according to one study (Kamil and Lane 1998) is that at least 96% of the text on the World Wide Web is expository! If we are going to prepare children for this world, we need to be very serious about teaching them to read and write informational text. It may not be difficult to convince children of the need for this, as we draw their attention to the informational text that surrounds them in their world.

3. **Informational text is preferred reading material for some children.** When researchers investigate what kinds of texts children like to read, they've found something that probably doesn't surprise you—different children have different reading preferences. Some children seem to prefer informational text, some seem to prefer narrative text; many don't seem to have preferences for any particular genre. For those children who do prefer informational text (children Jobe and Dayton-Sakari (2002) call "Info-Kids"), including more informational text in classrooms may improve attitudes toward reading and even serve as a catalyst for overall literacy development (Caswell and Duke 1998).

4. **Informational text often addresses childrens' interests and questions.** Regardless of whether a child tends to prefer infor-mational text, when the topic of an informational text is of particular interest to a child, their reading is likely to improve (Schiefele, Krapp, and Winteler 1992). Not surprisingly then, approaches that emphasize reading for the purpose of address-ing real questions children have about their world tend to lead

to higher achievement and motivation (Guthrie et al. 1996). Including more informational text in classrooms may help us address more childrens' interests and questions.

5. **Informational text builds knowledge of the natural and social world.** By definition, informational text conveys information about the natural and social world (Duke 2000). Reading and listening to informational text can develop children's knowledge of the world around them (Anderson and Guthrie 1999; Duke and Kays 1998). This in turn can promote children's comprehension of subsequent texts they read (Wilson and Anderson 1986), as higher background knowledge is associated with higher comprehension. Including more informational text in our classrooms may help us develop more knowledgeable and skilled readers.

6. **Informational text has many important text features.** Studies of informational texts, even those written for young children, identify a number of text features that may support children's overall development (Purcell-Gates and Duke 2001). For example, informational text often includes a great deal of technical vocabulary. Indeed, studies show that parents and teachers attend more to vocabulary and concepts when reading aloud informational text (Mason et al. 1989; Pellegrini et al. 1990) than when reading narrative text. Informational text may be particularly well-suited to building vocabulary (Dreher 2000; Duke, Bennett-Armistead, and Roberts 2002). Informational text also includes a number of graphical devices; learning to read those may support children's overall visual literacy development.

For these and other reasons, it's clear that informational text makes promising positive contributions to children's literacy and content area development. But what actually happens to children's literacy development, achievement, and motivation if we do include more informational text in their classrooms over a period of years? It is to address precisely this question that I have been conducting a research project in the state of Michigan. In this project, a group of first- and second-grade teachers were provided with money and support to diversify the genres their children read, wrote, and listened to. The goal was to include approximately one-third informational genres, one-third narrative genres, and one-third other genres, such as poetry and procedural text. They worked to do this not only in classroom activities, but also in their classroom libraries and on classroom walls and other surfaces. Another group of teachers was given similar money and support to increase text exposure for their students, but were not told that the study concerned genre and did not increase children's exposure to informational text to the same degree. Another group of teachers did not receive money or support during the data collection phase of the study. Schools were assigned at random to have teachers in one of these three groups, and in each school, one class of children was followed through first and second grade in the classrooms of participating teachers.

We are still analyzing the data we have collected in this study, but we are almost finished with our analyses from first grade. So far, the data indicates that there is no harm in including more informational text in first- and second-grade classrooms (as those who think young children can't or don't want to interact with informational text might predict there would be). On the contrary, the study shows benefits to including more informational text at these grade levels. For example, children in the experimental group (the group asked to diversify genres) were better writers of informational text at the end of first grade and didn't experience the same drop in (positive) attitudes toward reading that we saw among children in the other groups. Children who entered the experimental classrooms with low literacy knowledge had better reading comprehension at the end of the year than did similar children from the other classrooms—exposure to informational text seemed to help "level the playing field" for these children. (See Duke, Martineau, Frank, and Bennett-Armistead (2002) for a report of first-grade results of the study. See Duke et al. (2002) for a description of practices used by some of the first- and second-grade teachers, as well as other research-based practices for using informational text.)

As you can see, there is a growing body of research about informational text in early schooling. But there is still much that we do not know. We do not know nearly enough about which approaches to including informational text in classrooms are the most effective, and for which students at which grade levels. We don't know enough about how children's knowledge of informational text develops over time. We don't know enough about how including a great deal of informational text in schooling impacts children in the long term, or how it affects different children. We have a lot to learn in research. I hope that you will look out for new research in this area and work to make sure your practices are consistent with the research. I also hope that researchers will look carefully at the practices you develop in your classrooms. So often, the practices that researchers find to be most effective are originally developed in the classrooms of great teachers.

2

Thinking as a Reader and Writer of Informational Text

MARGARET MOONEY

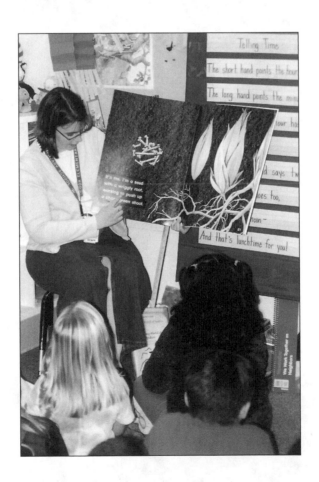

The timeless saying of "the more I know, the less I know" is especially true in my understandings about reading and writing and certainly applies to my thoughts about the reading and writing of informational texts. Just when I think I understand one minuscule aspect of how we read and write, the acceptance of that new knowledge triggers a domino effect on everything I thought I knew and had locked away securely. It causes me to face more doubts and accept resulting inconsistencies in my beliefs and practices, and so the continuous learning cycle triggers more moments of discomfort—followed by the joy of new learning and . . .

One of these major learning cycles was initiated by some musings around claims that certain resources were as effective for the teaching of writing as they were for the teaching of reading. My thoughts were also influenced by my involvement in a state reform process in the name of reading but, in reality, a re-evaluation of the nature of learning and teaching. I began by questioning the reading–writing claims. I reflected first on my own reading and writing and my beliefs and practices as a teacher of reading and writing, and then I matched my understandings alongside those of researchers and other practitioners. The ensuing questions included some chicken and egg queries for which there were no clear answers such as "How much reading are you doing as you write?" and "Do we learn to read before we learn to write?" But the answers to other questions brought a blinding realization that practices and beliefs are dancing to different tunes and beats. Some of these questions follow:

> If reading and writing are similar, why do we teach a particular skill in reading at one time of the year and the same or comparable skill in writing at another?

> How can we say being able to use a skill in writing is an indication of the level of understanding if we are not providing guided practice in writing as it is acquired in reading?

> How much time do we spend planning our reading lessons? Do we give the same care and passion to writing lessons?

> Do we expend as much energy and enthusiasm in guided writing as we do in guided reading?

> How much of a student's report on science or social studies is dependent on their competencies as readers and as writers?

I cannot quantify the discomfort I experienced as I pondered the clear message that our expectations of *writing* have been as great, if not greater, than of reading, but that reading has received the greater portion of our resources of finance, time, personnel, and enthusiasm. Suffice it to say that I suffered enormous guilt when I thought of the catch-up work some of my colleagues would have had to do in their students' writing once they had left my care and guidance (or lack of it).

The next domino to fall came as a result of my work as a series author developing a resource for reading and writing through the clichéd "range of genre." At that time, the diet of material used in the early grades was mainly fantasy fiction, usually six pages of repetitive text with a noun change and a final page carrying both the punch line (often humor requiring the teacher to interpret for the young readers) and a complete change of structure. Being a New Zealander, working

Figure 2-1   Success with informational texts depends on competencies in both reading and writing.

in Australia, developing material for a much wider market including the United States, soon taught me that our imaginations and therefore our ability to enter the fantasy world created by another author, have a strong cultural perspective. I became more aware of how many children, especially those labeled remedial readers, gravitate to the nonfiction sections of libraries and yet how often these children are steered toward the picture book section from which the informational books have been culled. Children pore over detailed diagrams showing the intricate workings of machines, can often "read" the labels, and retell their learnings with interest and understanding beyond that gained when reading texts requiring an unfamiliar kind of imagination.

Internalizing my findings led me to reconsider what and how I read and write. My bookshelves show a definite preference for informational texts in those books I have bought, whereas those given as gifts have been almost exclusively fiction. This could mean that family and friends are trying to bring balance to my reading habits, but I believe it an indication that many people place more value on reading for pleasure through fiction than through nonfiction. But informational books dominate the knowledge and understandings we need in order to be a literate person and a functioning member of society.

I found I also write more freely and with more enthusiasm when conveying information or ideas and opinions about informational topics than when endeavoring to transport my readers into an imaginary world. Thinking beyond my writing preferences, I am reminded of the weight of informational writing that is required to be considered literate, both within the education system and the world.

And so the search continued and still continues, with dominoes engendering deeper thought and revelations that cause me to wonder how I could have been so blind to truths and such startling evidence. What have I learned and what do I now know and believe? I should rephrase that as "currently know and believe" because I am sure that writing this will cause yet more amendments and raise more questions for consideration.

Reading has been defined as "writing in the head" as we turn print into language. Writing is reading through the pen as we turn language into print, knowing where we are in the act of recording our ideas as we see and read the letter patterns grouped into words, phrases, and sentences in captions, labels, codes, and texts. When reading, we turn print into language as we predict, discuss, and confirm. When writing, we turn language into print as we record for our readers to turn it into language. The phonological, syntactical, and semantic strategies we use to decode and comprehend as we turn print into language also help us record language as print. The sequence may change, but the questions we ask (consciously in our early stages of development or, for more competent readers, when the challenge is great) can help us record our thoughts with the same accuracy and fluency as they do in reading. The questions I encourage students to use when meeting an unknown word in print are:

What letters and sounds can you see and hear? (Phonological)

What kind of word will it be? What will the word do? (Syntactical)

What will the word tell you about? (Semantic)

The same questions asked in reverse order help a writer who is having difficulty choosing an appropriate word or with the spelling of a challenging word.

What will the word tell about?

What kind of word is it?

What letters and sounds can I see and hear?

In both reading and writing, the cue used to make predictions about the likely content, form, style, emphasis, or vocabulary cannot be used as confirmation. The other two cues need to come into play in order for the threads of meaning to be maintained. The three-pronged approach to decoding is critical in informational texts because technical language and generic noun construction may increase the difficulty level when composing text as the information is read or recorded.

Encouraging students to make links between reading and writing caused me to also think about the similarities and differences between the way we read and write fiction and nonfiction (or informational) texts. In fiction, a writer engages readers in dialogue through the nature and actions of characters conveyed through the mood and plot. In nonfiction, the writer endeavors to write with a credible and authoritative voice to cause readers to buy into new information and opinions to increase their knowledge and to influence their beliefs about themselves, their worlds, and other worlds. These differences influence both the reading and the writing of particular texts—fiction or informational text.

When reading fiction, one tries to gather up all the clues, details, and incidents the author has recorded in order to see the entire setting and participate fully in the incidents as if the plot was unfolding in our presence. The information we gather from the setting, plot, characters, and incidents in a piece of fiction is added to what we already know and used consciously within the context of that reading or book. It does, of course, add to all further reading and our knowledge of similar events. Reading informational text requires a more selective approach with the key strategy often being deciding what is not necessary for our purpose, either at the moment or in the probable future. In informational text, we are usually gathering and selecting information from a number of sources—diagrams, labels, captions, footnotes, and often, from more than one book about the same or similar topics. Each piece of information may expand, reflect, or compete with what we have gained from other parts of the text, book, or other books. The new information from each source has to be assimilated into our background knowledge as well as compared and contrasted with the other sources. And within the classroom context, students usually need to make a decision about how they will use, reshape, or represent the relevant information.

When reading fiction the normal pattern is to gather the new ideas and information as we move through the book sequentially. (Although some readers turn to the end of the book first and then fit the incidents into the solution of the problem or climax of the piece.) Readers of informational text usually make more circumspect choices about the way they will read a particular book. Often these choices are influenced by the purpose of the reading. Only some sections may be read according to the current purpose or interest. The most inviting sections may be read first or an overview gained through the illustrative material or chapter summaries may precede a more detailed reading. Or, sections relevant to a particular aspect of the topic identified through the table of contents or index may be the only ones read.

A reader of informational text usually makes more decisions before they begin reading—decisions about what and how they will read a particular book—than a reader of fiction needs to consider. Some of these decisions are made according to the purpose, perhaps to validate an opinion or understanding, to add to a knowledge base, or to consider another perspective. Other decisions will be about the style of reading appropriate for the purpose. For example, to *scan* if looking for a particular reference or section, to *read carefully* and slowly if reading new material that may prove challenging in content, language, or style, to *reread* if needing to remember details to complete a specific task.

The writer of informational text needs to know how to control, or at least influence, the way a reader gains the author's perspective during the actual reading. This will depend on the depth of the writer's understanding of how a reader dips and delves into informational texts and on knowing the range of appropriate textual and illustrative features and techniques. The writer needs to be able to twist the pen to support or extend the basic text, knowing when to nudge the reader to pause, to refer to other parts of the text, to assimilate the same information presented diagrammatically, or to reread a section to gain the intended emphasis.

Although authors of informational text accept that some readers may intend to read only those parts relevant to a particular aspect of the topic, they want to persuade the readers to read the book in its entirety. So, while every section can stand alone, there must be a link between chapters and sections, creating a desire within the reader to continue dialogue with the author. Fiction writers often end a chapter at the tension point of an incident, knowing this will hold their readers and keep them committed to reading to the end of the book. Chapters in information texts often "round off" with a summary or re-emphasis of the author's bias, requiring a strong theme or issue to underpin the complete text.

In order for young readers and writers to understand the similarities and differences between reading and writing and between fiction and nonfiction, teachers need to provide explicit and frequent models and demonstrations in shared reading and writing and focused intentional instruction in guided reading and writing.

Guided reading is an instructional approach where the teacher selects material and asks questions or provides prompts that will cause the repeated application of recently acquired skills or provide practice for those currently being learned. Every lesson should cause students to:

> Use phonological, semantic, and syntactic cues to ensure
> accurate, fluent, and expressive oral and silent reading;

Comprehend and internalize ideas and information presented in text and, where appropriate, in illustrative material;

Consider the act of reading as well as what has been read.

Guided writing is an instructional approach where the teacher observes, prompts, and monitors the students during the act of writing, ensuring the skills and strategies learned in reading are applied to produce accurate, fluent, and expressive writing.

Through the guided approach, the teacher is able to:

Observe students being responsible for reading and writing on the first reading or composing of a text, intervening only when meaning has been lost or other challenges are causing frustration;

Encourage thought and effort beyond the superficial, ensuring each student participates with maximum effort;

Observe and identify the strategies students employ consistently and appropriately, reminding students of known strategies and encouraging the use of new ones;

Adjust expectations and support according to each student's potential and encourage the use of alternative strategies and skills for greater efficiency or depth;

Encourage skills learned in reading to be used when writing and vice versa;

Encourage discussion about why and how the text was read or written;

Maintain an appropriate working pace and provide prompt support when necessary;

Assess continuously and individually during the act of reading and writing as well as provide immediate feedback on effort and the product.

The support, guidance, and encouragement provided during a guided lesson enables each student to:

Receive immediate feedback on effort and achievement;

Feel encouraged in independence but supported in difficulty;

Figure 2-2   Ali Taylor, McMinnville, Oregon, finds that guided writing groups accelerate development.

Practice strategies and skills within an encouraging though expectant environment;

Explore newly acquired strategies and skills and hone or extend known ones;

Work at optimum level and consistent pace;

Be a supportive and responsible group member, listening and responding to the opinions of others at a similar stage of development.

Whatever the approach and level, it is imperative that instruction in the early grades does not cause any unlearning in later stages of development. The knowledge and strategies established in beginning readers and writers should form a secure foundation for refinement and extension in all subsequent learning and applications.

One example where unlearning is required is the common definition of nonfiction. Young readers are often told that nonfiction contains facts, as in *truth*. One only needs to be reminded that books with titles such as *The Miracle 24-Hour Diet, Make a Million Dollars Without Moving from Your Home,* and *Little Red Riding Hood* would be found in the nonfiction section of the library to realize that a different or wider criteria is necessary. Nonfiction material contains as many elements of bias and persuasion as any fictional work. The reason for reading and writing nonfiction should be to consider another person's ideas and information. Our definition should focus on the informational aspect, thus emphasizing the reader's role in determining credibility and truth and selecting what needs to be considered in more detail or remembered.

Another example where unlearning is often required is the so-called "story" under a young child's picture. At the same time that we are calling their one-sentence labeling a "story," we are telling them in reading that a story has a beginning, middle, and ending. By calling the former a caption, we are not only introducing them to accurate terminology, but are avoiding confusion.

The reading and writing of informational texts requires a sharp eye and a sharp pen. A young child's innate curiosity and wonder about the world around them provide a rich resource to use as a guide in their journey through the printed word. Our challenge is to ensure their life-long travels in reading and writing open new vistas, extend their understandings, and widen their experiences as they explore their world and the worlds of others.

3

The Power of Informational Texts in Developing Readers and Writers

BRENDA PARKES

Informational texts make up a large and ever-increasing amount of what we read and write as we go about our daily lives. These texts permeate our workplaces, our travel, our recreational pursuits, and our everyday routines. As a result, by the time they enter school, children will already be familiar with some of the everyday informational texts routinely used by their families and themselves in their homes and communities. They will have observed how texts such as advertising, billboards, lists, letters, emails, greeting cards, and road signs are written and how and why people use them. In many cases, children will be confidently use informational print for themselves as they recognize words and graphics on the packaging of their favorite foods and frequently purchased items in stores; recognize logos and print that relate to places where their families and friends work and play; identify the traffic signs and billboards they see on the way to places they regularly visit; and "read" the names of favorite stores or fast food outlets. Many children will also be experimenting with writing for all kinds of purposes such as combining strings of letters and some words to write notes and make lists; adding their names to cards, letters, and emails for family and friends; and labeling their drawings, paintings, and constructions. Many youngsters know that reading and writing are personally meaningful and purposeful even before starting kindergarten.

Yet despite the proliferation of informational texts, the important role they play in our everyday lives, and the experiential background all children have with these texts, research shows that until very recently, informational texts have played little or no part in the early years of literacy instruction. Despite an increased awareness of the value of including informational text in early literacy programs, the time allocated to their use remains minimal (Duke 2000). Not surprisingly, when students are introduced to science and social studies textbooks for the first time in third grade, many of them experience some difficulties reading and comprehending these new kinds of texts. The skills and strategies they have learned through working only with fiction do not transfer seamlessly to informational texts. Not only are the students faced with having to understand new content, but also with additional ways of accessing and processing the information.

There are many good reasons to include informational texts in the literacy program from the first days of school. As previously stated, all children bring life experience of these kinds of real-world high-interest texts simply by living in the world. The photographs used to illustrate these texts are interesting and engaging, representing the world as children know and recognize it. This allows them to step into the pages by visualizing and making connections to their own experiences. This is particularly helpful to students whose first language is not

English, for it helps them use what they know and understand in their primary language to build bridges to comprehending and using the new. Together, the factual information and photographs in informational texts enable all children to draw on their personal knowledge and experience together with their curiosity about their world to raise questions, make comments, and contribute to discussions. Some children may bring background experience from television and other media, from conversations with family and friends, and others have developed understandings from books or firsthand experience. But all can take an active role in some way.

Many of the topics in informational texts match what children are learning in the content areas of science, social studies, mathematics, and technology. These relevant reading materials deepen and broaden the children's understandings and knowledge as they explore, for instance, how different authors write about the same or similar topics and how they choose to illustrate their material. This shows that textbooks are about the stuff of the real world.

In addition, children can begin to develop a sense of the way texts in particular content areas are organized and how the information is shaped. For example, authors of social studies texts frequently use primary sources including letters, journals, and diaries to allow the reader to hear firsthand the voices of the people whom they are reading about and use photos to help readers visualize and make inferences about what life was like then. Or, how words and phrases can signal the passing of time and timelines can summarize information. Students can learn how authors of science texts use primary sources including field notes, diagrams, drawings, and experiments to help readers construct meaning. They learn that many science texts are structured around the processes of observing, classifying, measuring, inferring, and communicating.

Early experience with informational texts builds a foundation for lifelong learning and an understanding that reading is meaningful and purposeful. It generates further purposes for reading, extending how, what, and why children read. Through the exploration of informational texts, young readers and writers can also deepen their understanding of how and why writers write. If the children experience explicit demonstrations and take part in discussions about the author's purposes and decisions during read aloud, shared, and guided reading, the texts can also act not only as catalysts but also as models for chil-

Figure 3-1   Early experiences with informational texts build a foundation for lifelong reading and writing.

dren's own writing. These demonstrations allow children to see how purposes are set, language is used, content organized, and information presented through written and visual features such as headings, diagrams, tables, charts, and glossaries.

Through their close observation and analysis of children's writing, teachers are able to provide support through guided writing lessons that help children take further steps toward independence.

What Features of Informational Texts Do Students Need to Recognize, Understand, and Use?

To effectively read and write nonfiction texts, children need to know and understand how to draw on the following elements to select, sift, comprehend, synthesize, and analyze information. They need to know how these features are interdependent and combine to communicate information. It is essential that children are able to use this knowledge to present information in different ways for different purposes.

What Features of Informational Texts Do Students Need to Recognize, Understand, and Use?

LAYOUT FEATURES	WHAT STUDENTS NEED TO KNOW
• table of contents	• how to quickly and efficiently glean information and make decisions about what to read
• index	
• glossary	
• headings & subheadings	
• bold, colored, or italicized print	• why authors use these to highlight text
• charts, diagrams, maps, drawings, and other forms of visual literacy	• how to access and interpret the information in concert with written text
• photographs	• how to look for detail, draw inferences, and connect with written information
• captions, labels, and continuous text	• how to read and integrate this information

LANGUAGE FEATURES	WHAT STUDENTS NEED TO KNOW
• language choices and text organization	• how the author's purpose and subject matter affect these
• specialized language	• the different ways this is introduced and explained
• nonfiction language structures cause/effect problem/solution compare/contrast description sequence	• why authors choose to convey particular information through these structures and the language that often identifies their use
• organization of content	• how to recognize and use organizational patterns to predict and confirm

What Reading Strategies Do Readers Need in Order to Process Informational Text?

It is essential that students receive explicit instruction in strategies for processing informational text and that they have sufficient time and opportunity to practice and apply them. These strategies include:

- Setting purposes for reading
- Making connections with prior knowledge and experience
- Integrating cues from written and visual text
- Predicting, checking, monitoring, amending, and confirming from multiple sources
- Using appropriate strategies to decode unfamiliar vocabulary including specialized content vocabulary and terms
- Skimming, scanning, browsing, rereading, and adjusting reading pace according to the reading purpose
- Summarizing information
- Analyzing and synthesizing information
- Noticing, interpreting, and using text structures
- Questioning the author and the text
- Using organizational features quickly and efficiently

How Do Guided Reading and Writing Support Learning About Informational Texts?

Guided reading and writing provide highly supportive settings and are powerful vehicles for explicitly teaching a range of effective strategies for independently reading, writing, and comprehending increasingly challenging texts.

Because the teaching occurs in a collaborative small-group situation, the reader can draw on support from the text, teacher, and other group members. This social situation enhances reading and comprehension as the teacher guides readers to share their knowledge and experience as well as their strategies for making meaning. The different combinations of written and visual text found in informational guided reading books provide a rich resource for discussion and encourage the use of appropriate strategies. The teacher chooses a text or topic that is carefully matched to the reader's current needs, interests, and understandings, ensuring the reader or writer is assured of a successful, enjoyable experience.

The availability of an extensive range of guided reading books focusing on the content areas allows a wide choice of appropriate topics. While some students experience difficulty reading content area material in lengthy textbooks, the shorter guided reading books allow them access to the specific content in more manageable and varied ways. More importantly, these books have been designed for guided reading as "considerate text" to support children as they learn how to access and process information. In turn, the guided reading lesson builds background to support understandings about the content of textbooks and provides strategies and experiences for reading and understanding them. Within a guided reading lesson, there are many opportunities to focus explicitly on working toward independence with some aspect of text, while also practicing those parts of the text already under control. Each part of the guided reading lesson provides authentic purposes for implicitly and explicitly modeling and engaging students in applying and consolidating strategies for reading and comprehending informational text.

Guided reading also provides many opportunities for students to develop valuable understandings about writing informational texts. These include:

- Using informational text structures such as problem/solution
- Cause and effect, sequence, description, compare/contrast
- Writing different kinds of captions
- Developing main ideas and supporting detail
- Including diaries, journals, and field notes to add authenticity and voice
- Developing diagrams and flowcharts

Over the years much has been written about the symbiotic relationship between reading and writing. Suggestions for making strong links between reading and writing include:

- Inviting and supporting dialogue about the writers craft during informational book read alouds

- Continuing the demonstrations and dialogue with the expectancy of increased involvement and understanding during shared reading and writing
- Providing further demonstrations and increasing the expectancy of independent use during guided reading and writing

Teachers can systematically make the links between these complementary language processes transparent, and in doing so, maximize support for developing readers and writers.

4

Critical Literacy Through Guided Experiences with Informational Texts

LINDA HOYT

As the volume of world knowledge continues to grow, it is essential that we challenge our children from the earliest ages to read critically. As readers of the future, as well as the present, they need to consider perspectives, point of view, accuracy, and relevance of information. When learners adapt a stance of critical literacy, they can more easily see the persuasive and biased tones inherent in advertising, letters to the editor, promotional brochures, and even bulk emails! They can question research reviews and wonder if the numbers and studies were selected to make a certain point or chosen to represent a broad base of thinking on the topic. As writers, they learn to be cautious in their research, deliberate in separating fact from opinion, and steadfast in their search for clear communication.

Children who have experienced the benefits of critical literacy instruction notice the author's perspectives in historical recounts and pause to wonder if another perspective might bring different understandings. They wonder what kind of research a writer conducted or reviewed to develop an informational text . . . and if the research was adequate. They wonder in a persuasive piece if the author has held an open mind to both sides of the argument before taking a stance. In a scientific piece, critical literacy would lead them to consider the accuracy of facts and whether the text and the picture are both supporting factual understandings.

Guided reading and guided writing with informational texts provide a setting to carefully support and encourage critical literacy. Numerous books on the same topic can be read to support discussion, enhance the ability to see different perspectives, and to check for accuracy of information. The small size of the group ensures that students will speak and be spoken to more often and that there will be probing questions addressed to learners of all levels of achievement.

When students are given only one text on a topic and are told to read it and answer questions, they naturally infer that this text represents "truth." They believe that they are being asked to study and learn from this text because it is important and factual. Why not have students engage in cross-dimensional reading and thinking by reading multiple *resources on the same topic*, discussing points of view, and information learned? This would increase time with text, deepen content knowledge, and cast the learners as co-researchers with the teacher.

While most of us do not have the scientific background or level of world knowledge to catch all potential misunderstandings our students derive from text, we can create a culture of critical literacy with

Figure 4-1   Reading multiple resources on the same topic
encourages critical thinking and broadens understanding.

a strong focus on reading multiple sources and questioning content and perspective.

The writings about Christopher Columbus have become classic examples of misinformation spread as truth. For centuries, children have grown up celebrating Christopher Columbus as the discoverer of North America, even though we knew that he didn't *discover* America. It was already richly inhabited by people with sophisticated cultures and a possibly more livable lifestyle than that of Europe at the time (*Atlantic Monthly*, March 2002). However, if students read about Christopher Columbus, about the Vikings who explored the area two hundred years earlier, and then read about the highly developed cultures and agricultural talents of the native North American tribes, the conversation that develops can be rich with multiple perspectives and an aura of reflective data gathering.

When this broadening of perspective is applied to a study of pilgrims, for example, students can take statements from a text, consider what each means, then generate questions that reflect multiple perspectives and implications far beyond a simple recounting of dates and events.

We Read	We Realize This Means	We Question
The Pilgrims landed and started to build homes.	The natives had to share the land. There was less space.	What happened to the wild animals that lived here? Were the natives able to hunt for food? If the Pilgrims built houses, did the natives leave? Is this text telling us both sides of the story?

Learning to Present Both Sides

Students also benefit from taking a statement and then listing support from two different perspectives.

Example:

YES	STATEMENT	NO
The wood helps people build homes and businesses.	Loggers should be able to cut down old growth trees.	Animals lose their homes. They need the trees for habitat.
Loggers would be out of jobs if they couldn't cut the trees.		Those trees took 100 years to grow.
When trees are cut the undergrowth has a chance to develop, which is healthy for the soil.		Trees control water and erosion.

Thinking Critically

Reader _____   Date _____

Sources Read _____

Agree	Statement	Disagree
_____	_____	_____
_____	_____	_____
_____	_____	_____
_____	_____	_____
_____	_____	_____
_____	_____	_____
_____	_____	_____
_____	_____	_____
_____	_____	_____
_____	_____	_____
_____	_____	_____
_____	_____	_____
_____	_____	_____
_____	_____	_____

After reading, discussing, and thinking, I believe that _____,

should happen. I support my thinking with the following: _____

_____

_____

_____

_____

_____

Shifting Perspectives

A Sample:

THE PROBLEM:	POSSIBLE SOLUTION:

Schools Need More Money ⟶ Increase Taxes

Argument For:

Schools need books.

Kids are the future!

Argument Against:

Taxpayers don't want to pay more.

Taxpayers think teachers could be more careful with money.

_____

_____

_____

_____

_____

_____

_____

_____

Conclusion _____

_____

_____

_____

_____

_____

_____

_____

_____

_____

_____

_____

_____

Additional Possibilities

Read a nonfiction book on a topic then read a fiction book related to the same topic. Compare the information in each.

Emergent Level

Children enjoy guided reading selections such as *Fly, Butterfly* (Brenda Parkes, Newbridge) and *Caterpillar Diary* (Rigby). Then listen to *The Very Hungry Caterpillar* by Eric Carle and *The Butterfly* by Patricia Pollacco as read alouds. What did they notice about the books? Are all books factual? Do they tell the same things about butterflies? What was the point of view in each? Who told it?

Developing Level

In guided reading, read books such as *The Biggest Bear* (Lynd Ward) and *Blueberries for Sal* (McCloskey), then read factual books on bears. Compare the way each author portrayed the bear. Were the actions of the bears in the two fiction stories realistic based on what we learned about bears?

Fluent

Read a variety of informational books on the Underground Railroad and Harriet Tubman. Then read *Barefoot: Escape on the Underground Railroad* (Edwards); *The Secret to Freedom* (Vaughan); *Under the Quilt of Night* (Hopkinson). Discuss how facts were addressed in the fictional works. Did the fiction works bring out further questions about the realities? How did the facts in the informational books support your understanding of the fiction? What was the perspective of each author? Were they focused on the runaways, those helping them, or on the slave owners? How might each text have been different if the perspective changed?

Examples of Further Explorations for Fluent Readers

- Read a book on an historical event such as the Civil War. Who do you think was telling the story? What was that person's perspective? What other perspective might there have been?

- Read a historical fiction piece. Try to see the story through the eyes of each main character. What do you notice as you change roles?
- Meet in teams to discuss topics of interest to your school.
  Discuss the questions from the perspective of the principal, the teacher, your parents, a student.
  Write about your thinking from the various perspectives.
  Should the lunchtime be longer?
  Should the school day be longer?
  How could students help the school to run more efficiently?
  Should the parents do the yard work at the school to save money?
- Read a variety of advertisements in the newspaper and magazines. What do you notice about the perspective of the writer? Who is the intended audience? Is the ad telling the truth?
- As part of our study of the American Revolution, you will be writing a journal entry that should cover the events of one week. You need to decide if you will be writing as
  ☐An American   ☐An Englishman   ☐A Native American
  ☐A Frenchman
- Please include facts from history as you know them but be clear about your thoughts and feelings from the perspective of your character.
- As we learn about eagles, you will be writing and drawing about eagles. Please decide if you are taking the perspective of the eagle or the eagle's prey. Then reflect your perspective in your drawing and in your writing.
- Read advertisements and then try the products. What do you think of the claims made in the ad? Are they true? How else might you investigate?

PART 2

Tapping into Informational Text Structures and Text Features

Informational text features such as captions, headings, bullets, and a table of contents lend important support to our readers and give writers tools for making their messages more clearly understood. Learners who are aware of these features and use them consciously during reading and writing have been proven to remember more and understand more deeply. Similarly, the six text structures commonly found in informational texts are important structural elements that our students need to understand and watch for in their reading and as they construct pieces of informational writing.

The chapters in this section bring attention to the role that text features and text structures play in learner understanding. As you move through this section you will experience "theory to practice" as Margaret helps us look at the *whys* of text features and the remaining chapters take you right into the heart of daily application.

5

The *Why* of Some of the Features of Informational Texts

MARGARET MOONEY

Guided reading provides students with an opportunity to understand the purpose as well as the nature of features in informational text. These features make the text accessible and highlight the important points in informational texts. Students can then apply these features in their own guided writing with teachers offering guided supervision and support. Some of the key understandings in informational texts include the purposes and format of the title, table of contents, blurb, index, glossary, diagrams, and tables. Following are notes on key features of informational books that students should understand:

Captions

a comment under, above, or near an illustration that:

- explains the content or choice of the illustration
- summarizes part or all of the text
- draws the reader's attention to key information
- provides an example of a point made in the text
- presents another point of view
- anchors the text in reality
- expands the reader's view of the text

Figure 5-1   Text features are powerful support systems to emphasize during guided reading and guided writing with informational texts.

Table of Contents

the author's plan showing organization of the book that:

- allows the reader to map a sequence or selection for reading
- provides an overview of the contents and the ways the topics are treated
- shows main sections and subsections
- shows how sections or topics are linked
- enables browsers to decide whether or not to delve further

Index

a detailed view of the contents that:

- provides quick access to a more detailed overview than offered in the contents page
- indicates the author's emphasis
- enables the reader to cross-check information
- enables the reader to gather more information about a topic

Figure 5-2   Text features such as an index and table of contents help readers locate information quickly and efficiently.

Diagrams

a visual portrayal of information that:

- provides a more detailed or a simplified view of a text or part of a text
- brings key points to the reader's attention
- shows relativity between elements
- explains position or nature of objects
- shows sequence
- provides an inside view of a cross-section

Glossary

a mini-dictionary within a book that:

- explains the author's understanding of vocabulary and terms in the specific context
- provides a pronunciation guide
- provides the reader with quick access to meanings of words that may be unfamiliar
- keeps the reader committed to a text that may appear difficult because of its technical vocabulary

Tables

a summary of more than one set of information that:

- highlights similarities and differences
- provides a large amount of information in a short space
- provides an example of information referred to in the body of the text
- causes readers to see things another way

Blurb

the publisher's message on the cover or in the text's opening
pages that:

- tempts the browsing reader to dig deeper
- introduces the topic and its treatment
- provides an overview of the content and writing style
- helps the reader set a purpose for reading the book

6
Coming to Terms with a Table of Contents

JODI WILSON

"Oh, goodie," squealed Kaycee, a zealous second-grade reader, "Another book about animals!" As she prepared for our morning guided reading lesson, Kaycee pulled up her chair, bulging book bag in hand, and readied herself for the introduction of a new book. Kaycee is one of those students who can keep you enthralled with what seems to be an endless knowledge of each creature in the animal world. Kaycee talks the language of a zoologist. Every Monday morning she watchs *Animal Planet* as she fills her book bag with "easy, just-right, and challenging but interesting" books for the week. Her choices are often informational texts.

Kaycee has been smitten by expository text. Her reading appetite had fueled a need in our guided reading group to include nonfiction selections. It became clear that using Kaycee's interests would be key to propelling her forward. On days when my selection for the guided lesson had been a fiction title, Kaycee's enthusiasm waned. She would quickly read through the text once, slide it to the side, and then dive back into her book bag for a more inviting book on wolves or spiders. Kaycee's reading behaviors helped me to look differently at my text selection. I thought my careful planning always provided these young readers with a quality text that could be used to demonstrate and support the use of lifelong reading strategies. But my thinking was changing and I began to ask myself these questions:

- Why was it that I choose fiction for my students to read so often?
- What is my own reading appetite?
- Why was it that my teaching library was heavily weighted with oodles of fiction?
- Why was it that our school book room was overflowing with an enormous collection of narratives, fairy tales, and historical fiction, yet the nonfiction section begged to be noticed with its sparse number of book cartons and titles?
- How many times had I stood and watched as young children pulled a book about frogs or volcanoes from the shelf?

These questions opened my eyes to what my ears had been hearing for some time. Children want and need to be immersed in expository text. Today's children live in a world of visual literacy. Kids need to know how to read, construct, and interpret multiple types of text to be successful in their everyday lives. As an educator, I knew that I was crossing a bridge in my delivery of literacy instruction. I had come to understand that children must have ownership of strategies that will support them as they "learn to read and read to learn" all types of text, but most importantly, those from which they can gather and use information.

So informational texts became the genre of choice for five eager second-grade readers. No longer was Kaycee the nonfiction guru because now Jessica, Emily, Karlie, and Alissa had joined her in pro-claiming that nonfiction books "rock." Knowledge of wolves, animal homes, and pets was solid among these avid readers and their reper-toire of good reading strategies bloomed as they devoured book after book. Initially, the strategies they had used on fictional text provided them with a scaffold for success on this newly discovered genre. Soon, however, they began to see how merely skipping a word or finding a little word inside a big word was not always the most efficient way to extract meaning from the text. They needed more strategies.

As I analyzed the books that held special appeal for these children I realized patterns were emerging. I remembered reading in Steven Moline's book I *See What You Mean: Children Using Visual Information* (1995), that readers need to understand the "gateway" of the text they have chosen to read. He defines the gateway as the point at which a reader enters a text. As readers of "stories," our gateway is very different from the gateway for a text we are reading to glean information.

> There is more than one way to read a book. We can read it from front to back, intently, leaving nothing out. We can browse through the pictures. We can search for one or two facts, picking out only the straws we need from the haystack of information. We can scan, sample, skip and skim. How we read depends on our purpose for reading.

As I observed my readers and analyzed the text introduction of their newest nonfiction title, it dawned on me that I had been mod-eling finding the gateway of fiction and expository text as one in the same when indeed they were very different. I had also failed to model the importance of determining the purpose of reading. Jessica approached a book by reading the cover, locating the title, skimming over the title page, glancing at the photograph on the right-hand side of the page, and then beginning to read the stacked text on the left. I knew that if I had put *Little Red Riding Hood* or *The Three Little Pigs* in her hands she would have read those texts in the very same way. If she had a purpose for reading, it remained in her head.

My eyes roamed around the group at the table. They loved reading, but did they know *why* they were reading? They read every book that they picked up in the same way—cover, title page, pictures to text, left to right, top to bottom, start to finish. I knew I had to teach them how to distinguish between "reading for information" and "reading for story" and, more importantly, how readers launch their reading by knowing their purpose, for example, to learn new information, to find answers to a burning question, or simply for pleasure.

The patterns I began to notice in the text included the following:

- The topic or ideas was usually singular in context, such as wolves or animal homes, and had high kid appeal. They were also topics that kids can easily connect with by using their prior knowledge.
- The layout followed a pattern. On the left-hand side of the page, the text was stacked with four to six sentences. To the right, a colorful photograph framed with a border provided support for content-specific vocabulary. The simplicity of these texts supported young readers.

Because the layout was so predictable, I realized I needed to find selections that provided support but moved the children's thinking forward. Their journey as expository readers would be paved with complex, sophisticated text features. It was time to provide them with some new reading roadmaps for success.

I sought quality informational texts that supported my guided reading group at the word level and matched their interests, yet challenged them through text features and page layout. My hunch was that these young readers' minds were ready to be opened to the multiple ways readers can find their text gateway.

Looking through the expository selections in our book room, I found a single topic text, with kid appeal, on pets—a perfect segue from the previous books that we had read on wolves and animal homes but with new challenges. The page layout of the text was very different from anything the children had read previously. The title page was followed by a simple table of contents, represented by small cartoon pictures of pet possibilities. The icons were randomly scattered about on the page, with no visible page numbers. On closer inspection, I realized the same icons had been used to indicate matching pages of pet content. I sensed that once explicitly taught, this would be a good support. "Did my group have any understanding of a table of contents? Did they understand that by using this text feature a reader could zigzag through the text, dipping from one section to another, propelled by their interest, and searching for answers to their questions?"

All of a sudden, I was looking at the book with very different eyes. Questions kept popping into my head. "How do I help my students scaffold the challenges?" "How can I help the students distinguish between reading fiction and informational texts?" Other text features that emerged in my review included: titles on each page, a supportive photograph of the pets, text organized in two paragraphs on the left page, a bulleted list of pet needs on the right, and a concluding supportive photograph.

I read Jane Hansen's book *When Writers Read*. In teaching children to write, Hansen reminded us that to write, one must learn to read like a writer. That is, a reader must be able to analyze the text, take it apart, and wonder as the author of those words did as they scribbled words on the paper whether they were successfully creating meaning and understanding for the reader. So if that were true of a reader of fictional text, I wondered if the same were true for readers of informational text? "Did these expository readers need to be able to read and analyze like expository writers?" Moline's thoughts on readers and writers of graphic design elements meshed with Hansen's. I concluded that readers need to know that text layout is deliberate and intentional and that readers use layout conventions to organize information and support their reading. They do this by determining what is important in the text and making conscious decisions about what they need to remember. Usually, the design enhances a reader's comprehension.

I had many questions in my head and a new focus in mind as our lessons continued. We revisited previously read nonfiction selections. The children began to compare the patterns in and across the books.

"I get it. They are all the same," Karlie exclaimed. "The photographs are always followed by words on the next page and they let me know more about the animals."

Emily chimed in, "Yeah, that makes this book really easy to read."

"How do you read this book?" I asked. "Do you have to start with the beginning page and read it from front to back?" Heads were nodding around the table.

"I always read my books that way. I don't want to miss a thing," Kaycee declared. Heads nodded in agreement again!

As I introduced the new text with all of its challenges, I invited the students to think beyond the words and to think about *why* the book was as it was. I began to model for them how, as a reader of expository text, I ask myself, "Why do I want to read this book? What am I hoping to learn? What information do I have in my head that I can use to help myself understand more as a reader? How is this book laid out? Why did the author place a photo here beside the words and how will it help me as a reader?" I told them, "Good readers talk to themselves as they choose books. They ask questions; they have their own opinions; they predict and go in search of answers. The information that we want to learn dictates how we choose a nonfiction text." I laid the next text beside our earlier selection of informational texts. "Is the text format for these books the same? What is different?"

With guiding questions, the students began to explore the new book on pets. They immediately noticed the bulleted list and how the animal icons matched the content of each page. They saw the bold print of the title headings and questions the author posed at the back of the book. The time they took to explore the book helped them begin to understand some of the special features of informational text, including how an author organizes information to help a reader know where to begin to read.

"So where do you want to start reading in this book?" I asked once again. The students responded with different names of the animals. "And is it O.K. if Karlie starts on the section about dogs because she is thinking about getting one and Jessica reads about iguanas because she finds them interesting?" This time they gave an emphatic "YES!" These readers had discovered the power of determining their own gateway. They could state their purpose for reading and begin to read this text in a zigzag fashion.

"This table of contents isn't very good," Alissa stated.

"How come?" I asked.

"Well, the tables of contents that I've seen in other books usually have page numbers so I know where to find some stuff. If the author had put numbers by these pictures, then this book would be even easier to read." Alissa's prior knowledge of using a table of contents brought us all back to another discussion. With some coaching and questioning from me, it was decided that they wanted to add more to this table of contents to make it more efficient to use for readers. Out came the white sticky note tape, sticky notes, and pencils. We added page numbers to the corresponding pictures and added other content features of the text on a sticky note in their book. With their new reader's gateway knowledge in hand and an expanded table of contents, each went off in search of a new reading partner to share her expertise. I sat back and watched. These hungry readers were engaged in purposeful learning that they created for themselves. They were hooked!!

The table of contents lesson became the gateway for many more nonfiction books to come. Kaycee became vigilant in her use of text features. One day as we were warming up by rereading a couple of old

Figure 6-1   A student at work on a table of contents

favorites from her book bag, she brought our attention to the fact that two of our books did not have a table of contents.

"So what do you think we should do about that?" I asked and silently hoped that these girls would say, "I think we should make one and add it to the book." Which is exactly what they did say. Each reader chose a book, grabbed small pieces of paper the size of the inside cover, and created a table of contents, rereading passages, deciding on the important topics in each book section, and checking other nonfiction titles for ideas for the layout of their table of contents. With a "new set of eyes" to take their prior knowledge to a deeper, more thoughtful level, these readers were well on their way to demystifying complex expository text they would be reading for years to come.

These readers of informational text were not only reading like graphic designers, but they were creating and putting their text designs to work as well! Reading like writers AND writing like readers.

Figure 6-2   Kaycee, Emily, Jessica, Karlie, and Alissa proudly display their newly composed table of contents for an informational book of their own choice.

7
Using Text Features as Tools for Learning

JAN MCCALL

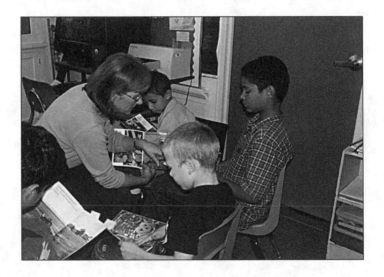

Informational text has many features designed to support readers in maneuvering through resources. When readers expect these features and know how to use them, they can move in and out of informational texts, selecting pages that will provide the most assistance on their topic, connecting pictures and text blocks, and accessing information with efficiency and comprehension.

Commonly occurring features might include those identified in the following chart. This chart can be used to plan or monitor coverage of some of the key features of informational texts as well as be used by students in reviewing resources and the support features they offer.

Informational Text Features
Print Features, Graphic Aids, and Organizational Aids

TITLE OF BOOK	Bold Print	Colored Print	Italics	Titles	Headings	Labels	Captions	Bullets	Fact Boxes	Sidebars	Diagrams	Flow Diagrams	Size Comparisons	Magnifications	Photographs	Cross-Section/Cutaway	Tables	Graphs	Charts	Timelines	Maps	Table of Contents	Introduction	Supplemental Inform.	Index	Glossary	Pronunciation Guide

Figure 7-1   *Jan McCall's text feature chart.*

© 2003 by Linda Hoyt, Margaret Mooney, and Brenda Parkes from *Exploring Informational Texts*. Portsmouth, NH: Heinemann.

8

Understanding Text Structures

LINDA HOYT AND TERESA THERRIAULT

It has been well-proven that students who understand text structures anticipate content and have higher levels of retention than
students who do not (Hoyt 1999; Harvey 1998). The following text
structures are worth examining to determine their common attributes and to ensure that learners experience all forms from the
perspective of a reader as well as a writer. Once students become

familiar with the basic organizational structures, they can more easily predict challenges in text, identify language features, and incorporate critical attributes into their own writing.

Knowledge of these core structures and signal words provides support to readers so they can better anticipate language and features of each structure during reading. As writers, they understand what the reader expects and can craft their writing to match the structure being used.

Knowledge of these structures can also help us make correct choices of graphic organizers. Organizers are supposed to assist readers and writers with print. When the graphic organizer selected does not match the structure of the text, the organizer actually presents a challenge to the reader/writer.

Teresa Therriault, reading specialist and consultant from San Diego, California, has merged the work of Fountas and Pinnell (2001), Harvey (1998), Hoyt (1999), and First Steps (1995) into one useful grid that students and teachers alike may find to be helpful.

Text Structures in Informational Texts

Text Pattern	Definition	Key Words	Maps/Webs	Examples of Texts	Examples of Texts
Description	Descriptive details about characteristics, actions, etc.	descriptive adjective and words like: on, over, beyond, within		*The crocodile is the master of deception in water. It stalks its prey and then swiftly closes in for the kill.*	*Goose bumps make me shiver. I get little bumps on my skin. They look like sesame seeds.*
Problem/ Solution	Sets up a problem and its solutions	propose, conclude, a solution, the reason for, the problem or question		*One problem to resolve in crocodile watching is transportation. How can an observer get close enoug . . .*	*Goose bumps make me shiver. But they disappear as soon as I cover up with a jacket or sweater.*
Time/Order Chronological	Gives information in order of occurrence	first, second, before, after, finally, then, next, earlier		*Archaeologists have helped us to understand that the evolution of the crocodile began with . . .*	*Goose bumps make me shiver. First I get cold. Then I shake all over.*
Comparison/ Contrast	Looking at two or more items to establish similarities/differences	while, yet, but, rather, most, same, either, as well as, like and unlike, as opposed to		*The power of the crocodile is like that of a monstrous machine. With one lunge it can . . . Compared to the alligator the crocodile . . .*	*Some people get goose bumps from fear. Others get goose bumps when they are touched emotionally.*
Cause/Effect	Give reason/explanation for happening	because, since, if/then, due to, as a result, for this reason, on account of, consequently		*We observed the crocodile as it stalked a raccoon . . . As a result of the noise we made, the rabbit bolted . . .*	*Goose bumps make me shiver. When the temperature drops below 45 degrees, my skin crinkles into goose.*
Source of Information	Dept. of Education Western Australia, First Steps, 1995.	Fountas, I., and Pinnell, G. 2001. Guiding Readers and Writers Grades 3–6. Portsmouth, NH: Heinemann.		Hoyt, L. 1999. Revisit, Reflect, Retell. Portsmouth, NH: Heinemann.	Harvey, S. 1998. Nonfiction Matters. York, ME: Stenhouse.

Figure 8-1 *This material was contributed by Teresa Therriault.*

TEXT STRUCTURE	EXAMPLES	ATTRIBUTES	KEY WORDS
Descriptive	Reports Summaries All about books Poetic descriptions Arguments Public information statements Letters to the editor	• Factual statements • Subject-specific vocabulary • Attempts to build a setting, visuals reader • Time is not implied • Present tense often used	adjectives, strong verbs
Persuasive *Subset of descriptive		• Makes a particular point from one point of view • Tries to convince the reader • Attempts to develop loyalty May show both sides then make a statement of belief	*because, furthermore, however, therefore* (Continues)

TEXT STRUCTURE	EXAMPLES	ATTRIBUTES	KEY WORDS
	Advertisements	• Phrases, titles, joining statements, used to promote or to sell	*I believe, because, since, based upon, you should, buy now, join in, understand, on the contrary, you need to, therefore, from my point of view*
Problem/ Solution	Factual accounts that state a problem and a resolution	• Fact or opinion may be included	*a reason for, because, when, if _____ then, to solve, a problem, the solution, conclude*
Time Order	Biography My trip to Mt. St. Helens Observations of plant growth News articles, current events Historical recounts Diary Autobiography	• Descriptive language • Shows passage of time • Chronicles events • Retell real life • Who, what, when, where, why	*finally, before, next, then, in addition, after, first, second, before, earlier, later*
Compare and Contrast	Shows how at least two things are alike and different. May use metaphor, simile, analogy, description		*although, compared with, unlike, similar to, different than, however, like, likewise, the difference between, but, and yet, however, as opposed to*

(Continues)

TEXT STRUCTURE	EXAMPLES	ATTRIBUTES	KEY WORDS
	Could include then and now accounts Comparison diagrams and photos		
Cause and Effect	How pulleys work Why rain causes erosion Why the tiger is in danger	• Explanations • Present tense language • *Because*, and time-order words often included	*makes, causes, because, if, then, results in, so, creates, when, since, on account of, due to, therefore*
Directions	How to build a bridge How to make chocolate chip cookies Steps in conducting a science experiment Rules to a game Finding the square root	• Uses short sentences or phrases • Lists of materials, steps • Directive language: *stir, mix, measure* • Order is listed with numerals: sequence words such as *next, then, first*	*first, then, second, third, finally, after, next, gather*

(Continues)

Selecting Books to Represent Core Text Structures

	Books to Use with Primary Students	Books to Use with Intermediate Students
Descriptive		
Problem/Solution		
Time/Order Chronological		
Comparison/Contrast		
Cause/Effect		

PART 3

Understanding Informational Text Through Guided Reading

There is no recipe for guided reading, but the opinions and practices presented in this section all emphasize the importance of students making meaning for themselves. A teacher's role is to show students how to make meaning and to ensure that students are developing strategies that can be carried over to other topics and applications.

The contributors in this section focus on the questions and strategies they use through the small-group organization of guided reading and on the nuances of gathering, selecting, and applying information.

Guided reading goes well beyond the literacy period—it is an inherent part of all day and every day in the classroom. Reading is a tool or vehicle for accessing information and ideas, whatever the subject label. In the same way, guided reading is not a single approach for a certain period of the day. It is as much an attitude as a strategy— a belief that no one can make meaning for anyone else; the reader must be the one who connects with the author. The teacher of guided reading is continually watching the connections made between reader and author and is constantly changing gears through questions and prompts to keep that dialogue clear and continuous.

9

Guided Reading with Informational Text

LINDA HOYT

Guided reading is a small-group instructional model in which children actively read and problem solve their way through a text. The teacher scaffolds the reading by building content knowledge, vocabulary, and language on the topic. Margaret Mooney in *Reading to, with, and By Children* (1990), states that in guided reading "the teacher uses questions and comments to help children become aware of resources within themselves and in the text which will enable them to overcome difficulties" in reading (46). This approach to reading instruction results in learners who develop independent reading strategies that can be easily transferred to other texts. When this model is directed toward informational texts, children have explicit support in *reading to learn*, while they are *learning to read*.

In guided reading with informational text, teachers and students prepare for reading through discussion, previewing the text, and relating experiences to the content. Reading is done independently while the teacher circulates and listens to individuals. Support is provided for the content being learned as well as for the challenges of the print.

With emergent readers, the text might be read all at once. With proficient readers engaging in longer, more complex texts the reading would be paced so that students read fairly short passages then stop to discuss, reflect, and prepare for the next section of reading. In texts that take several days to read, students might read some sections of a text independently while other sections of text would be targeted for guided reading. After reading, the teacher leads a conversation on the content learned, on reading strategies used, and teaches a lesson on the finer points of language or phonics.

Guided Reading with Informational Text Makes It Possible to:

Learn about the world, while learning to read

Scaffold content-based vocabulary and language before reading

Preview text forms and structures before reading

Develop strategies specific to reading informational texts

Teach to specific needs of the group members

See students as individuals

(Continues)

Guided Reading . . . *(Continued)*

Explicitly teach reading strategies

Support fluency with text

Support self-monitoring of comprehension

Listen to individuals read quietly so the others are not disturbed while they read to themselves

Investigate many forms of informational texts

Connect reading to topics studied in science and social studies

Teach phonics, word knowledge and extend vocabulary

Check on self-monitoring behaviors such as:

  using multiple strategies for dealing with unknown words

  rereading to confirm meaning

  self-correcting when meaning has been distorted

  adjusting reading rate

  hesitating

  checking for picture clues

  using boldface headings, captions, and other text features

  responding to reading through laughter, personal comments, or nonverbal gestures

Questions to Ask Yourself . . . When Reflecting on Guided Reading with Info Texts

Teachers need to continuously evaluate text selections and instructional supports. Some reflective questions might include:

  Is the text too easy or too difficult?

  Is the concept load too heavy?

  Is this topic interesting to these students?

  Does this reader have a wide array of strategies for unknown words?

(Continues)

Questions to Ask Yourself . . . *(Continued)*

Is the student reading too fast or too slowly?

Are the readers making connections with the text?

Which teaching points would be most helpful to these readers at our next guided reading session?

Am I teaching or reinforcing good reader strategies every time we meet?

Do students have opportunities to discuss the attributes of different text structures?

Is meaning the key focus, even when you are teaching strategies and skills?

Are you assessing reading within informational texts as well as fiction?

Assessment in Informational Guided Reading

Because guided reading groups are small, I can closely observe learners. I watch as they interact with the text, searching for observable clues that they understand and can apply strategies. I can observe their ability to use picture clues, to ask questions of the content, to apply letter/sound correspondences, and so on. When I assess in both fiction and nonfiction, I can check for the learner's ability to transfer strategy use across genres.

I am careful to listen to individuals read during guided reading. I ask them to read quietly into my ear so that they don't disturb others who are reading to themselves. During this time, I take running records, record substitutions made while reading, and tally strategies being used while individuals read to me from informational texts.

While listening to individuals, I try to detect use of informational text features such as headings, table of contents, etc. It is important to get a broad view of learner development and you cannot do that if you are conducting all of your assessments in fiction.

Listening to individuals read is precious time as it allows me to see, even within the small-group context, how each learner is progressing. This individual time is also my opportunity to assess the match between

Figure 9-1 Spiders, *(Newbridge) It is important to take running records and assess strategy use in informational texts such as these.*

Figure 9-2 Our Journey West *(National Geographic)*

the reader and the text. As I listen to each reader, I have a perfect opportunity to determine if the text is at the just-right level, if it is too challenging, or if it offers so few challenges that the reader doesn't have an opportunity to really stretch and utilize the full range of strategies. This also gives me the opportunity to check for content understanding and determine if the reader needs support in making meaning while reading.

Guided Reading Is for Readers of All Ages and Phases of Development

Guided reading is often associated with primary students or those who need additional help with reading. I believe that readers of all ages benefit from small-group instruction that focuses on features of text, strategies for making meaning, and a closer look at how text works.

Finding Resources for Guided Reading

Any informational text can be used for guided reading. Resources could include information books that are leveled and designed for guided reading. Great guided reading lessons can also include: textbooks on science, social studies, or health, newsmagazines, menus, brochures, recipe books, the newspaper, student-authored informational texts, resource books, informational picture books, and so on.

A Possible Structure for an Informational Guided Reading Lesson

Warm-Up

- This is a time when students browse through familiar books or text sections that have been previously read. The goal is to reflect, revisit memorable portions of the text, savor strong visual images, or focus on the craft of the author.

- The warm-up can occur as the opening of the guided reading group or as an independent task before the guided reading group convenes. If you choose to have students warm up before the group meets, it is often helpful to ask them to mark an interesting point, identify a reading strategy they used, or share a challenge they have identified in the text. If they mark the place with a sticky note, they are better prepared to share with the group.

Activating Prior Knowledge That Relates to the Content to Come

- The goal is to activate prior knowledge on the topic, present concepts that are critical to understanding, and activate vocabulary. This could take the format of a brief discussion, a word sort of critical words, a retell of previous sections, or a hands-on experience related to the learning. The critical goal here is to bring concepts and vocabulary into a state of readiness so learners are assured that the text will be meaningful.

Minilesson #1—Strategy Instruction

- Select only one teaching point per lesson. While the possibilities for teaching points are endless, it is critical to select a teaching point that is targeted to the needs of this group of students. Demonstrate how the strategy works, provide practice, and then make it clear that you expect them to implement the strategy while reading. It is important to:

   √ support understanding of the topic

   √ demonstrate and explain the use of a good reader strategy

   √ focus on text structure or text features

- Explain that you will be asking them at the end of their reading to share their attempts to use the strategy or their observations about the text structure.

Minilesson Possibilities

GOOD READER STRATEGIES	TEXT FEATURES	LITERARY ELEMENTS/DEVICES
Using beginning/ending sounds	Directions	Using specific language
Chunking words	Signal words	Word choice
Prior knowledge	Compare/contrast	Descriptions
Making connections	Time/order	Voice
Identifying important ideas	Articles	Leads/endings
Creating visual images	Textbooks	Simile/metaphor
Making predictions	Captions	Power verbs
Retelling/summarizing	Boldface headings	Passage of time
Using prior knowledge	Newspapers	Imagery
Making substitutions	Table of contents	Writing titles
Backtracking	Index	Headings
Context clues	Glossary	Figurative language
Self-questioning	Info poetry	Point of view
Shifts in reading speed	Diagrams/charts	Stereotype
		Inference

Interaction

- This is a quiet reading time when students read *independently,* never in round robin format.

- While students read to themselves, the teacher can move around the group to listen to individuals or pull students aside for brief reading conferences. This is a very good time to gather a running record, record substitutions, or tally strategies used. Before students begin reading, establish a guideline for early finishers. I usually ask early finishers to reflect on the text, looking for outstanding passages, high-quality descriptors, particular points of interest, and so on.

Reflection

The reflection has two components:

1. Reflection on the passage.

   - What do you think about the reading today?
   - Were there any parts that were particularly interesting?
   - Were there any parts you found confusing?
   - How might we summarize the most important points?
   - Were there any vocabulary words you found challenging?
   - How did you deal with the challenges you faced?
   - Were there any strategies that worked particularly well for you today?

2. Reflection on the reading strategy of the day.

   - How did you do at using _____ (the strategy presented in the minilesson)?
   - Can someone share an example of using the strategy today?
   - How might this strategy be used in science or independent reading or in other kinds of reading?

Minilesson #2: Language Study

- Select a dimension of language study that is relevant to the needs of the group. Depending on their needs, you might ask group members to break some words from the reading into syllables, create lists of high-quality verbs and adjectives from the passage, make a list of words that start with a particular sound, use a prefix, or engage in a "Making Words Strategy" (Cunningham and Hall1998). (The word study can often be completed at a center or as an independent activity after the close of the guided reading session.)

Guided Reading with an Article

Resources: *Weekly Reader, Time for Kids, National Geographic for Kids,* daily newspaper, and so on.

Warm-Up

Preview the text to get an idea of what we will be reading.

Activate Prior Knowledge

What do you know about magazine articles? What text features might we expect to see in an article? (captions, photographs, direct language, facts, short passages with headings, titles . . .)

What do you know about the topic of the article?

Word Predictions: List five words you think might appear in an article on this topic.

Minilesson: Captions

Captions can fulfill many functions. They can restate information, elaborate on the text, or explain details in the illustrations. Notice the captions during reading and be prepared to talk about their functions in this article.

Read/Interact

Personal, independent reading or partner reading

Reflect

What did you learn? What did you notice about the captions? How did they help you as a reader?

Language Study

Skim back through the text and find words with two, three, and four syllables each. Be prepared to share the words and what they mean.

Guided Reading with an Emergent Information Text

TEXT: *BUBBLES* BY BRENDA PARKES, NEWBRIDGE

Warm-Up: rereading familiar books

Activating Prior Knowledge: Provide bubble-making liquid tools for blowing bubbles. As children blow bubbles, engage them in talking about the bubbles. What do they see? etc. Guide the children in a picture walk through the pages of the book, eliciting language to describe what they see in the pictures. Some readers might benefit from identifying the words on each page that they think will be the most important.

Minilesson: *In* and *On*

In and *on* look a great deal alike. How can we tell them apart while we are reading? What should we watch for? How could we check to see if we were correct? How might reading to the end of the line of print help us to know?

Interaction

Individuals read to themselves, print matching their way through the pages. Encourage several readings to increase fluency. Small tape recorders might be used for readers to record their reading as they feel they have reached fluency with the text.

Reflection

What did you learn about bubbles? What was interesting? Did anything surprise you? How did you do with *on* and *in*? What helped you as a reader? What will you remember next time you encounter words that look a lot alike?

Language Study

Use magnetic letters to create the word *bubbles*. Use the magnetic letters to write a word that tells your favorite place to find bubbles. Draw and write about bubbles. What do you know about them? When have you had an experience with bubbles? Where could you find bubbles at home? What makes bubbles? Or, write directions on how to blow the best bubbles.

10

Teachers and Students Overcome Challenges

BRENDA PARKES

Regardless of whether the lesson is for a kindergarten or a fifth-grade class, guided reading lessons offer many opportunities for teachers to remind children of the strategies they have or are currently learning and to explicitly teach new ones. A guided reading session comprises three main interconnected parts: introducing the text, reading the text, and discussing and revisiting the text. When reading informational texts, the emphasis of each of these three sections is on gathering, analyzing, comparing, and synthesizing information.

Introducing the Text

In order to make sense of a text, readers draw on a combination of their personal experiences, what they know about the world, and their previous experiences with texts. The more a reader is able to connect previous knowledge and experience to the genre and information in the text, the easier it is to comprehend that text. The introduction to a guided reading lesson provides explicit demonstrations of different ways of making connections and focusing thinking on the topic. The teacher's introduction must maintain a delicate balance between providing enough information to get the reading started while still leaving substantial reading work for the children.

Introductions vary depending on the book, the group of learners, and the purpose for using the particular text at that time. Over time these multiple experiences provide students with many opportunities to develop strategies for accessing information and independently introducing texts to themselves. Informational guided reading books have a number of features that support the reader in getting an overview of content and deciding if the book suits their purpose. They also help the reader decide how much of the book they will read at any one time. These strategies include:

- drawing on relevant background knowledge to begin making connections with content and concepts
- noting the information on front- and back-cover text and pictures
- skimming the table of contents, index, headings, and subheadings

- setting purposes for reading
- recognizing and using text structure and organization such as sequence or comparative sets of information
- asking questions about the text
- gathering information from headings and subheadings
- browsing through the text to get an overview of the content and to find the different ways the author has communicated the information
- noting information in a chart, map, or diagram
- recognizing words or phrases that signal structural patterns

In the following extracts from a guided reading lesson the teacher is introducing the book *Big Digs* (Newbridge). Her main purpose for selecting this text is to provide the group with experience with the problem/solution structure of the informational text.

A Guided Reading Lesson

Introducing the Text

The book we're going to read today is called *Big Digs*. The United States has participated in three large building projects, The Panama Canal, The Hoover Dam, and one in Boston that is actually called the Big Dig.

As you skim and scan through this book, I want you to tell me the different ways that the author has organized information.

Ella: Well. There are lots of photographs.

Ben: And there are maps and captions.

Teacher: What page are you on?

Ben: Pages 17 and 24.

Teacher: How do these maps help us?

Elizabeth: They show . . . like . . . the location of the projects.

Teacher: What have you got Cody?

Cody: One of those working construction things.

Teacher: Has anyone any idea what you'd call that?

Ella: A blueprint or something?

Teacher: Could I call it a diagram?

Cody: Yes. It's another diagram, like on page 18.

Ella: On page 18 it shows inside the dam and right here it shows the outer and the surface part.

Teacher: So those two really go together . . .

Cody: When I visited the Hoover Dam before, looking down into this area my Dad told me that these little spinning things turned the water into electricity.

Teacher: So you can really connect with the Hoover Dam because you've been there before.

Teacher: What do you have here?

Nathan: Fact boxes.

Teacher: When I was reading this book the fact boxes were just my favorite because I love all sorts of trivia.

Teacher: Turn to the table of contents. I want you to look at the titles for pages 6, 14, and 22. If you think back to the blurb we read on the back cover and think how we skimmed and scanned through the book, how do you these titles relate to what we're going to read about? What do you think a shortcut through the jungle will be about? And what about "The Panama Canal"? And what does the title for page 14, "Taming a Wild River," make you think about?

Reading the Text

In a typical guided reading lesson the students work to independently use the processing strategies they already control as well as those they are still working on. As they read the text silently or in quiet voices, the teacher observes their use of strategies. These observations form the basis for discussion following the reading and for subsequent book choices. It also allows the teacher to provide just the right kind and amount of support to help a reader regain or maintain meaning when and where needed.

Figure 10-1　Careful observation during reading provides the teacher with valuable information about each reader.

Teacher: I want you to turn to pages 4 and 5. This will give us an intro-
　　　duction to the whole book so I want you to skim these pages.
　　　What are your thoughts?

Cody: You can see the machines they used to build the construction.

Teacher: You really used your picture clues. Did you read the caption that went along with the picture? Why don't you read that out loud to us.

Cody: *Digging is the first step, and careful construction comes next for projects such as canals, dams, tunnels and bridges.*

Teacher: So I think this book will be about digging. They had to dig everything.

Ella: You can tell by all the pictures and the covers.

Teacher: Did you learn anything from these paragraphs?

Nathan: It gives an introduction. It tells what the book is going to be about.

Teacher: And it answers the question, Why dig? Let's turn to the first chapter. Look at the beautiful picture on page 7. Read the text on page 6. I'm going to ask you what problems they had cutting through the jungle.

Elizabeth: When they tried to get around that jungle . . .

Cody: And it took a long time to cut through the jungle.

Teacher: What are the two headings on pages 8 and 11?

Cody: Facing problems. Finding solutions.

Teacher: Turn to page 12. What fascinated me when I read this book was the information that went along with the diagram. So pay attention to that. I want you to find three problems and the solutions that went along with those problems.

The teacher records anecdotal notes as she observes the students reading silently.

Discussing and Revisiting the Text

In this part of the guided reading lesson students revisit parts of the text to reflect on their learning and to communicate their ideas, feelings, and strategies through discussion and debate.

Discussion will first focus on their personal responses about content and style, connections they have made, and their initial understanding of the author's intended meaning. They may revisit parts of the book to find supporting detail for their discussion or to raise further questions. The teacher may also want to highlight some important aspect of the book in a brief, explicit lesson. Such lessons could include:

- focusing on how to comprehend information in a diagram
- how structural patterns organize and link the ideas in the text
- what inferences can be drawn from the language or pictures
- using problem-solving strategies for unusual or unfamiliar words in context
- summarizing and synthesizing information

When the students have silently read the chapter, the problems and solutions are discussed as the teacher records the information on a chart. She prompts them to draw on all sources of information in the text to support their responses and to "piggyback off" each others' comments.

Problems	**Solutions**
Yellow fever and malaria	Drained swamps
	Cleared tall grasses
Chagres River flooded and delayed digging	Built a dam
Where to put extra dirt	Built a dam

Teacher: What was the next problem?

Ella: The Chagres river kept flooding.

Teacher: So that was a problem? Why was it a problem?

Nathan: It delayed the digging.

Teacher: How did they solve this problem? What did they do?

Cody: They built a dam. They excavated the dirt . . .

Teacher: What does that mean?

Cody: Well. They got the dirt.

Teacher: Where did it all come from?

Ella: From the digging.

Teacher: And what was the problem with the dirt?

Nathan: It got in the way.

Teacher: So what did they do?

Nathan: They built a dam.

Teacher: So that dam actually solved the problem.

Ella: I have another problem. It's in the second paragraph on page 12.

Teacher: What was this problem?

Ella: The newly created Gatun Lake was 85 feet higher than the Atlantic Ocean.

Teacher: How would they solve that problem?

Ella: The answer was to build locks—a series of water elevators—to raise and lower ships to different water levels.

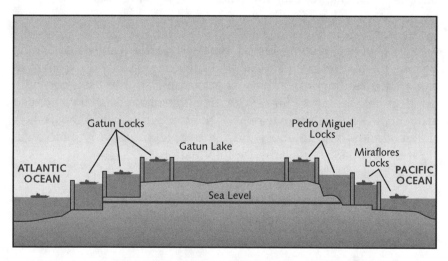

Each lock is like a big tub full of water, but the tubs have gates that open to let water and ships in or out. When water pours into a lock, it moves the ship higher. When water pours out of a lock, it moves the ship lower. In this way, ships pass from the lower level of the oceans to the higher level of Gatun Lake. Because of the twists and turns along the way, a ship that enters the canal from the Atlantic side leaves the canal 27 miles east of where it started! You can see this on the map on page 8.

Figure 10-2   Guiding children to use diagrams, labels, and other text features enhances understanding and develops independent problem-solving skills.

Teacher: Can you see that on the diagram?

Nathan: How does that work?

Teacher: If you look at your diagram on page 12 you'll see they had to build the locks. That way it was able to move from the low Atlantic up to the Gatun Lake and down to the Pacific.

As the teacher reads and explains the diagram, the group follow along in their own copy of the book.

The teacher continues to invite students to contribute problems and solutions. Her conversational prompts and questions ensure the students draw on meaning from all available sources and that all the students are actively involved in the reading and thinking. When all students have contributed to the chart, the teacher concludes the lesson by asking the group to turn to the table of contents and each choose which chapter they will read and make notes on to discuss in their next guided reading lesson.

The guided reading lesson can also be the catalyst for going beyond the text to extend meaning. This is an optional component of the guided reading lesson but one that can form the basis for independent but related reading and writing. Personal research could lead students to explore some feature of the topic in detail, compare how different authors write about the same topic, or use a graphic organizer to summarize or synthesize information.

11
Traveling in Depth

MARGARET MOONEY

Young children have an innate curiosity about the world around them. Small creatures, large objects, the way creatures move, and the workings of machines fascinate most youngsters. Guided reading of informational texts offers opportunities for teachers to nurture this wonderment and, at the same time, helps children increase their understanding of the benefits of reading to learn. When the teacher is an active group participant, expressing her wonder, questioning her thoughts, or asking questions of the author, she can elicit thoughts or enhance conversations within the group or even between the children and author. The teacher's comments can also highlight the important information and show children which facts are worth remembering. Ideally, the teacher models strategies good readers use to "travel in depth." Some of the comments I use in guided reading include:

> "Well, I never knew that. Will you read that again to help me remember it?"
>
> "I wonder how that could be/happen."
>
> "Have you ever seen such an amazing thing?"
>
> "I want to look closely at the diagram to see what else I can learn."
>
> "I was fascinated when you read about . . ."
>
> "Just think of that! How incredible!"
>
> "I need to go back and read that again. It was something new and I want to think about it."
>
> The author must have thought that was important because it is repeated here/in the caption."
>
> "Oh, at first I hadn't noticed how . . ."

Such leading comments often cause the students to reread sections or to scan illustrative material in order to "help the teacher out" or come to the teacher's rescue. I recall commenting on a sequence diagram in *Pineapple Pizza* (Drew 1997) and how quickly my student Faaletasi came to my aid.

Teacher: I did not know so many things happened in making a pizza.

Faaletasi: Well, you see, it is easy if you put your finger here (pointing to the top of the diagram) and just follow those pointed marks (arrows) you know what comes next. That's why those marks are there. You need to remember that next time.

On another occasion, when I had expressed surprise at the number of ants shown in the diagram of the ant nest, my student Brent quickly reminded me, "but the author said on that other page that there were thousands . . ."

One has to be careful not to overdo such comments, detracting from the thread of the text or from the children's responsibility of making their own meaning. The reader must decide what is important and worth remembering. As with questioning, the teacher's comments should moti-vate thought within the reader, beyond the text, and beyond the actual reading. And the effectiveness is dependent on the degree to which the book itself nurtures dipping and delving, skimming and scanning, and close scrutiny. Elaine Moss, writing in *Part of the Pattern* (1986) says:

> This is really what nonfiction books are about: opening your eyes to the world so that you see things that you otherwise would have missed. Because of *one* enthusiast's ("one" is rather important) enthusiasm you begin to be an enthusiast yourself. You begin to understand what you are looking at, to have what is commonly known as a *revelation* about the world. (This is what Freda Stark means when she talks about traveling in depth instead of traveling distances. What matters, she says, is that what you see shall reveal something new to you.)

One of the teacher's key roles during guided reading is to provoke thought so students will "travel in depth." While there is a place for the literal questions where readers can merely locate key words, phrases, or sections, the majority of questions should cause thought beyond the text, taking the readers to new depths of understanding. Questions should be framed to extend thought and not shut it down as happens when a "yes" or "no" response is accepted. This also happens when responses are accepted with a "yes"—the student may think he/she has done sufficient thinking to satisfy the teacher. It is important that stu-dents see questions as an aid to making the text accessible or to achieving full understanding. Some of the questions should be designed so that the responses provide information about the strate-gies used to select information as well as the information itself.

Thought-provoking questions will require the teacher to allow "wait" time (which research shows to be a minimum of five seconds) for the students to process the question and formulate a response. More time may be required if information has to be internalized or summarized or information from several parts of the text must be syn-thesized. This is also the case if sections of text need to reread to find the details necessary for a comprehensive response.

There should be a balance of questions asked at each stage of the lesson, of those about the information and its usefulness or application, and of those requiring an oral or written response. Balance

Figure 11-1   Thoughtful responses to reading may require a return to the text and sufficient "wait time" to encourage deeper thinking.

should also be a guide for the number of questions requiring responses and those causing the readers to ask more questions of themselves or of the text. If every question requires an answer for the teacher, the reading will be seen as an activity to please the teacher rather than to select information.

The following questions are designed for students working at a third-grade level and beyond but may be adapted to many kinds of informational text.

Before the Reading

Questions about the form of the text

What clues does the cover give about the way the author might present the information?

If this piece is an X kind of text, what feature do you expect to meet? What does that mean for how you will read this?

Read the blurb on the back of the book. What does that tell you about the form of the text?

What else have you read in a similar form? How will that help you as you read this text?

What text or book features might be included?

Questions About Reading Style and Pace

How much attention do you think you might need to pay to the text/illustrations?

We have determined this is an X kind of text. What will you need to remember as you read it?

How will the form of this piece influence the pace of your reading?

Do you already know a lot about this topic? How will that influence your reading?

What strategies are you likely to need to use?

Questions to Help Students Set a Purpose for Reading

What questions do you hope this book/chapter will answer?

What do you think the author wants you to focus on/think about as you read the text?

What questions did the blurb raise?

Look at the table of contents. What does that tell you about the author's intention for the book? Does that raise some questions in your mind?

Given what you already know about this topic, what will you be looking for?

What kind of information do you need in order to complete the assignment?

During the Reading

Questions About Strategies

Read until you gather one new fact. How can you check its accuracy?

Read the first page or . . . What do you notice about the vocabulary? What strategies will help you meet these challenges?

Which words are proving difficult? Are they nouns or . . . ? What letter patterns are you seeing that might help you?

Are you needing to slow down more than usual? What is causing that? What could you try?

Questions About Content

What kind of information are you gathering?

Are you finding much new information or are you confirming what you already know?

Where are you getting most of your new information from? The text or the diagrams?

What has been the most interesting/useful piece of information you have read so far?

Following the Reading

Questions About Reading Style and Strategies

Which parts were most difficult?

How did you clarify meanings of difficult words?

How did you work out unfamiliar words?

What kind of words cause the most problems?

Were you able to keep an even pace? If not, what caused the problem?

Did you need to reread many sections?

Questions About Content

Are there any parts that still confuse you or that you do not understand?

What pieces of information do you think are the most important/interesting/useful?

Do you think you have sufficient information to proceed with your task/satisfy your curiosity?

How did you check the accuracy of the information?

What bias did you detect?

Do you need/want to do further reading on this topic?

What have you learned that will probably be useful?

What do you think is the most important part of this lesson?

Do you think you will find more information when you reread this text?

Questions About Format

Was this a good format to use for this kind of information?

Did the format suit the topic and purpose?

Why do you think the author chose this format to present the information?

How else could the information have been presented?

Most of these questions can be used as discussion starters as well as for formative assessment that can provide information about the next appropriate questions to ask or offer guidance for the student. Thought-provoking questions motivate students to participate throughout the lesson and to pay more than cursory attention to *how* as well as *what* they are reading. Active participation can often provide more useful and detailed information about a student's progress than written activities or chapter tests. The feedback is immediate and suggestions for improvement can be practiced under the teacher's supportive guidance as they are noticed.

However, effective questioning is dependent on the teacher being very familiar with the text and knowing the competencies and interests of each student in great depth—and then being prepared to use these to formulate questions and to consider responses. Guided reading is responsive and intentional instruction at its best.

12

Oral Reading in Informational Texts: Let's Keep It in Perspective!

MICHAEL F. OPITZ

Thinking about using oral reading to better help students understand informational text? If so, here are five tips on how to keep oral reading in perspective when using informational text.

1.   Keep oral reading to a minimum.

While oral reading can be a way for you to help students understand text, we need to remember that in everyday life we use silent reading most often. In fact, one of the most important ideas we need to keep on the front burner as we engage children with text, especially informational text, is what accomplished readers really do when they read. Regardless of the text we are reading, we are rarely, if ever, expected to follow along as others read, waiting for our turn (i.e., round robin reading). This is why we would not expect children to do so when reading informational text.

But how will I know that they have read the text if they read it silently? How will I know if they comprehend the text? Both of these are valid questions that can be answered with this three-word sentence: Hold them accountable! For example, if students are to read and report on three facts they learned from the text and explain why they feel they are important ideas, they could use a form similar to the following one on the next page. This provides written documentation that students did indeed attend to the text and that they were able to glean essential information. If you want documentation that students listened and learned from others, you can have them write ideas using the bottom part of the form.

As with any effective teaching, students will need to see this modeled before they are expected to do it on their own. You might want to use this form as is or modify it to fit your own or the students' needs. Clearly, there is nothing magic about the number three!

2.   When oral reading is used, make sure it accomplishes a specific purpose.

Sometimes the best way for children to understand how to use a comprehension strategy, such as making connections, is through oral reading. For example, using a think-aloud procedure, you model how you make connections as you read. You then read a section of text to students and ask them to talk about the connections they made. The students read yet another section silently, which provides them with some practice. You also direct them to use a making-connection strategy. Finally, you ask for volunteers to read their section as others listen and then tell about the connections they made. Other students in the class are invited to share any connections that

Name: _____

Section: _____

Facts	Why I think this fact is important
1.	
2.	
3.	

Three ideas I learned from others:

1. _____
_____
_____
_____

2. _____
_____
_____
_____

3. _____
_____
_____
_____

Figure 12-1   This material was contributed by Michael Opitz.

Name:_____

Making Connections

Text	Connection I made

Figure 12-2   This material was contributed by Michael Opitz.
© 2003 by Linda Hoyt, Margaret Mooney, and Brenda Parkes from *Exploring Informational Texts*. Portsmouth, NH: Heinemann.

they made. As this example shows, oral reading is used by both you and your students to accomplish a specific purpose.

If you want documentation to show that students read and made connections, you might want to use a form similar to the one here.

3. **Use specific examples from the huge array of informational children's literature texts now available.**

How fortunate for the children we teach! My own teaching experiences have helped me to see that many children prefer informational text and find good reasons to read when they are able to select the book. Not only do these children stay engaged with the text, they also learn about different ways that texts are written.

4. **When children are expected to share with others, give them plenty of time to prepare.**

One reason that you might choose to use oral reading is to help students see that it is a means of communicating with others. This is usually accomplished through some sort of sharing. For example, at the conclusion of reading an article or a book, students might highlight one idea that caught their attention, read it aloud to interested others, and state why it is important. Or, each student might be given a different title and given five minutes to skim and locate one interesting fact. After these have been shared, students then trade books and repeat the process. One important point to keep in mind when expecting students to share information with others, however, is time to prepare. This preparation is essential, for it enables the reader to work out any problem areas before sharing with others. As a result of this preparation, the reader comes across as a fluent, confident reader who is mainly concerned with sharing information with other interested readers.

5. **Use specific questions to guide observations of children's oral reading and document what you hear.**

Oral reading can serve as a window into how children approach reading. Taking the time to look through this window can inform instruction if we know what we are trying to see. Questions such as the following can be used to guide observations. Rather than trying to use all questions, think about choosing the question or questions that best fit your purpose for the assessment. Once selected, your observations can be recorded on a form such as the one that follows the questions.

Sample Observation Questions

1. Does the child read for meaning?
2. What does the child do when meaning is not maintained?
3. Does the reader read with a sense of meaning, expression, and fluency?
4. How well can the child retell what was read?
5. How does the reader perceive the oral reading experience?

Figure 12-3

Class Observation Form

Focal Question: _____

Date: _____

Name of Student	Notes

Figure 12-4   This material was contributed by Michael Opitz.

Keep in mind that any new teaching strategy takes time to internalize. Persist until you feel at ease with it. And remember to take some time to celebrate your willingness to take some risks to make instruction better for your students.

13

Navigating Through Informational Texts

JANINE BATZLE

I rented a car recently, dreading the drive into Philadelphia on a dark, rainy Friday night. Having never been there before, the thought of an electronic navigator (GPS) in the rental car brought me a sense of comfort. I jumped in, punched in the coordinates of my destination, and took off. Driving along, the navigator began talking to me, "In the next three miles, you will make a right turn." I smiled. A few minutes passed, and The Voice said, "In one mile you will make a left turn." Before I knew it, The Voice and I were having intimate conversations, chatting along as my newly found friend helped me problem-solve my way through the traffic, on the rainy streets of Philadelphia.

Our students need an "internal navigator" of their own to support their interactions with the many types of informational text they are likely to encounter. When students know how to work through texts strategically, the topic of the text is much more accessible. Students will eagerly spend hours digging, perusing, curiously investigating, becoming thirsty information seekers when they know how to navigate a set path through the text.

When readers are independent they are able to do two things— adjust their reading strategies to match the texts they read and secondly, comprehend in deep and thoughtful ways. Readers who navigate well know where they should start on a page, what to read next, and how to work through the information presented in text features such as diagrams, timelines, subheadings, and captions.

When fiction is read, linear reading strategies are used. The book must be read in order. Skipping or jumping around in the text just won't work. However, when a newspaper or a magazine is read, non-linear reading strategies are used. Readers skim and scan, flipping through the pages and moving through the text, reading what's interesting or important to them. Students with an "internal navigator" have the ability to adjust their strategies to match the text they are reading, which supports them in becoming independent, self-directed readers of nonfiction.

Roadmap to Success with Informational Text

As we teach, we ask students to read, take notes, and synthesize what they've read. Then we scold them for plagiarizing! Without navigation strategies, they may unwittingly use copying strategies.

When I am teaching students to read informational text, I consider three types of strategies needed for comprehension:

1. **Strategies that help the student to navigate the text type.**
   I first observe and interview students to see how much experience they have had with the type of text I am asking them to read. If they have navigation strategies, then I move to comprehension and decoding strategies. If not, I start with what we read first, second, third, and how to read different types of text features, such as diagrams, graphs, etc.

2. **Strategies that help the student to comprehend and decode on the text type.**
   As students learn to navigate that particular text type, I observe and interview them to see if they have the comprehension and decoding strategies needed to get precise meaning. For example, students may competently handle decoding fiction text, but decoding subject-specific vocabulary in informational text may be challenging for them.

3. **Strategies that help to clarify and understand the topic content through writing.**
   When students can successfully comprehend what they have read, they can learn the content well. Students can use note-taking strategies, study skills, and summarize and synthesize without plagiarizing.

Strategy development takes time, so modeling, guided practice, and independent practice may be required over a 4–6 week period. When we only teach the topic of the text, it leads students to be dependent. When we teach the *reader* of the text, it leads to independence with any text.

14

Guided Reading in Mathematics

JERRY A. MILLER

A significant and welcome change in elementary curriculum during the past decade has been the introduction and use of a broader array of informational text to teach young readers. With the help of such useful reference works as Margaret Mooney's *Text Forms and Features: A Resource for Intentional Teaching* (2001), teachers have begun introducing young students to expository, procedural, persuasive, and poetic texts as well as the traditional fiction that comprised the bulk of elementary reading materials prior to this change.

In response to the need for primary-level texts of different types, publishers have flooded the market with colorful and appealing informational titles in many genres and on an enormous number of topics. As a result of these changes, primary students enter their middle years with a host of experiences in reading and responding to these individual text types. Then, they encounter their mathematics text!

Math texts present challenges for even the most seasoned reader. They are rich in complex content and concept matter and heavy with specialized and frequently confusing vocabulary. To make matters worse, the information is presented by melding a number of genres of text all on the same page.

On two pages of our district's fourth-grade math text, students are faced with the following:

- A narrative section, several paragraphs in length, about ants walking around a fountain
- An expository section giving key vocabulary and definitions related to measuring a two-dimensional surface
- A procedural section describing several scenarios and asking students to plan, measure, collect data, and perform multiple mathematical operations

Even if students are well-versed in each of the individual genres, we cannot assume they will recognize which is which when all three are mixed on two pages of text. If they do recognize the three text types, thoughtful discussion must still take place about how each type of text relates information, why the author chose to write each section in a different genre, and how we are going to read each section in order to gather the information we need to proceed.

Guiding students through their first reading of the math text can lead to increased comprehension of the mathematical content and will help students in future encounters with similar text layout.

Begin by reviewing the characteristics of each of the three most common genres contained in math texts: narrative, expository, and procedural. The chart on the next page, adapted from Mooney's work, will serve as a reminder to teachers.

Narrative	Tells a story. In the case of a math text, it gives a context in which to think about the concept, skill, or strategy under question.
Expository	Explains and defines ideas, concepts, and vocabulary. Mathematics texts tend to be exceedingly concept-rich and complex, requiring careful and repeated reading.
Procedural	Describes a particular setting and question or procedure that will require use of the mathematic skills and strategies under investigation.

Ask students to use sticky notes to mark the three individual sections in their texts. On the notes, students may jot down the text type, speculation as to why the author chose it for this section, and information specific to the unit under study (in this case, measurement.) These notes then become the focus of a prereading discussion that will support readers in working their way through the text during the remainder of the session.

Where's the Math?
The purpose of this activity is to:

- Focus student attention on math vocabulary
- Generate common understanding of math vocabulary
- Increase depth and breadth of math vocabulary knowledge

Materials Needed:

- Math textbook
- Highlighter tape

  Or

- Copied math pages
- Highlighter pens

1.   Individual students read through the math text (either book
     or copied pages) and highlight any "math words" they
     encounter.

2.   Teacher asks students to name a math word they have
     found and writes it on a wall chart.

3.   After a word is given, all students remove it from their list.

4.   This process is repeated until all math vocabulary is found
     in the text and put on the wall chart.

Follow-up Activities:

WORD SORT

Have students work in teams to identify three categories to
place all the words on the wall chart. Be able to justify the
category names and placement of words within them.

WORD LINKS

Have individual students or teams make a "word link" using
a graphic organizer. Then have them write a sentence
explaining how the two words go together.

Different Ways of Measuring a Two-Dimensional Object

area

perimeter

WORD LINKS

1.   Select words from the Word Wall that somehow go
     together.

2.   Write one word at the end of each arrow.

3.   In the center, explain how the words go together.

15

Quick Tips for Getting Started with Guided Reading of Informational Texts

CHERYLE FERLITA

It has been said that we do not know what our students will encounter as adults, but we do know that they will be expected to access information from many types of texts in an information-seeking and information-sharing world. And we know that guided reading situations offer an effective vehicle for helping students understand the nature of informational texts and how to use appropriate strategies for accessing their content. The following tips support the establishment and maintenance of successful guided reading sessions at all grades of the elementary school.

Tips for Establishing Guided Reading Groups

- Use reading levels of the students to select text at their instructional level. Examine supports and challenges in texts and be sure to have both in a text planned for a guided reading session. Too many challenges and the text will be difficult for the students to understand; too few and the students will not be working to their potential.

- Use an oral reading sample or an informal or formal reading inventory that includes an accuracy level, a fluency check, and an oral or written retelling.

- Use a student conference form to record reading strategies used, topic preferences, and new learning targets.

- Group readers according to a specific skill or strategy students need to practice.

- Group readers to facilitate language acquisition and conversation possibilities. This conversation will be the bridge to better comprehension and written communication.

- Observe carefully and continuously so students who are struggling get support as soon as possible. Change the group if needed, but make sure this is done judiciously.

- Ensure struggling readers are included as group members as often as possible, but provide time for them to preview the text and time for them to reread the text after the lesson.

Tips for Selecting Informational Texts for Guided Reading

- Get to know some of the titles, authors, and publishers that will suit the range of your students in both level and interest.

- Select text that students can verify with other sources or texts.

- Select factual text where students can verify accuracy.

- Avoid text that allows for misinterpretation of information.

- Avoid text that condescends to the reader.

- Select text of interest and immediate relevance.

- Select text with features appropriate for the genre, topic, and level. They may include charts, tables, graphs, photographs, diagrams, maps, webs, headings and subheadings, labels, captions, footnotes, references, and indices.

- Use some shorter texts and magazine articles, especially when introducing new strategies or textual and illustrative features.

Tips for Introducing an Informational Text in a Guided Reading Session

- Keep it short and focused on the content and format at of the text.

- Initiate conversation between the students and author through questions or activities that set the pattern of predicting and confirming.

- Listen carefully to the students' responses and dialogue as this guides the introduction and the amount of support probably needed during the reading.

- Ensure you model good conversation starters and ways of maintaining discussion and thought.

- Provide plenty of think time and establish cooperative strategies to encourage all to participate.

- Use graphic organizers that students can add to during and after the reading.

- Decide on a focus for the lesson based on student needs and interest, and develop the lesson so these strategies are practiced frequently.

- Discuss unfamiliar vocabulary and concepts.

Tips for Ensuring Students Understand as They Read

- Keep the group together by pausing at appropriate points to review or summarize what has been read and to set purposes for continued reading. This will help maintain the pace.

Figure 15-1   Students who take time to pause and reflect during reading are more likely to remember what they have read.

- Encourage students to reread the text as a follow-up to the lesson.

- Pay careful attention to the amount of new information the students will be responsible for and chunk the text accordingly.

- Give faster finishers a reason to dip back into the text to check facts, find responses to teacher-directed questions, or to revisit new ideas or sections they found interesting or new. They could make notes in a response log or flag it with a sticky note or coded card.

- Circulate and assist with one-on-one strategy talk where needed. It is important to honor readers by not interrupting the reading too much. Too many interruptions will interfere with comprehension.

- Encourage some oral reading—fluency and expression are clear indicators of comprehension.

- Listen to individual students reading short sections and discuss strategies they are finding useful, sections that are proving difficult, new information they are finding interesting or important, and questions the text has not yet answered.

- Making time for a brief discussion with each student is very important for those students who try to dominate the after-reading conversation as well as for those that do not want to add to the conversation at all.

Tips for Encouraging Responses Following the Reading

- Have students respond daily. This does not have to be lengthy or a formal assessment piece. Try to vary the format and/or focus.

- Discussion after the reading contributes to the success of the lesson by giving time for the teacher to assess and formulate teaching points for this or the next session.

- Encourage students who have located new or interesting information to initiate and perhaps lead the discussion.

- Discussion after the reading should usually include attention to a specific skill or strategy.

- Balance the type of responses between teacher-directed activities and those initiated by students, responses to the whole text or just a portion, long responses and shorter ones, responses determined before or during the reading, responses extending the postreading discussion, and, most importantly, a balance between oral and written responses.

- Responses can be kept in a response journal (perhaps a spiral notebook, a three-prong folder, or a three-ring notebook).

Tips for Determining the Time Devoted to a Text or Session

- A long lesson may mean the students are reading too much of the text during the session. Remember, nonfiction texts are full of facts and information that students need time to revisit and reread.

- Take the time needed to help the students understand the text and practice the reading strategies currently being acquired.

- If you spend too much time on one particular text or genre, it limits the amount and type of text students are exposed to during the year and they will associate informational text with lengthy sessions.

- It is important not to beat the text to death by pointing out all the skills possible within that one piece. Attention should only be drawn to those skills necessary to gain and maintain meaning.

- Going too quickly may also cause problems, because it does not allow students the time to practice strategies and internalize the concepts. If the reading takes on a very fast pace, it may be that the students are reading without comprehending or they need to be encouraged to think beyond the superficial. It could be that the text would be better read independently or a more complex assignment or purpose needs to be set.

16

Laying Foundations for Guided Reading Through Buddy Reading

NORMA GIBBS

Our students come from diverse cultures in a low socioeconomic area of the city, bringing a wide range of experiences in some aspects and few in others. So when teachers of our emergent readers began thinking about helping their students decode and understand informational texts, our discussions ranged far beyond the text or guided reading. It quickly became obvious that many things needed to be in place to support these students as they not only learned to read, but also began their journey of reading to learn about the world around them.

Many of the children are just acquiring English as their second language and do not have English labels for many of the things portrayed in informational books. So we took another look at our classroom environments, asking ourselves if they were conducive to promoting the use of language beyond the teacher–student interactions. We discussed ways in which the math area, science and writing centers, and other areas in the classroom could engender discussion and help students acquire and use language. One teacher recounted how the animal puzzles and farm and zoo construction toys in the math area had become useful resources during a read-aloud about farm animals. Having the opportunity to play with these toys and talk about them with the teacher and other students enabled the children to learn the names of animals—and for some to discover that baby sheep are not *sheeplets* and every large cat in the zoo is not a tiger.

The teachers considered other ways of helping these students develop background knowledge through language experience and shared reading experiences. They realized that it is easy to assume some of the essential vocabulary and concepts are in place. One teacher found that a book containing a simple recipe had no relevance as some of her students were used to ready-made meals. Following a simple recipe or procedural text became the basis for several language experience sessions. Another teacher told how he has built up a comprehensive photo and picture file of everyday events and objects found in the home, school, and the local community and how he uses it when reading to and with children or when introducing guided reading books.

The teachers discussed the benefits of storytelling and ways of extending the students' knowledge and use of language through increasing the number of opportunities within the school day to share personal experiences, songs, poems, rhymes, and finger plays. We discussed book selection and the need for total text and strong picture match through clear and simple illustrations as the children begin their learning-to-read journey.

However, all agreed that one of the most important features of a classroom to support students in learning to read and reading to learn would be reading *to* them. This led the school to implement a "Read To" program for five-year-olds as they entered school. The teacher would ensure that "read to" sessions were an essential part of the daily program and, for the first six months of school, the kindergartners would be paired with an older student who was a fluent reader. The older buddy would read to the younger student for fifteen minutes each day. After these daily readings, the younger student would be able to take the book home to share with family members. The younger student could also ask the buddy to reread the book.

The older students rehearsed for their very important role of reading to the younger students and participated in training that focused on techniques of reading aloud, showing their own interest and understanding of the books, engaging their partner in conversation and discussion about the book, and, most importantly, enjoying the experience.

The books purchased for the "Read To" program are high-quality picture books that relate in illustration and text to the children's

Figure 16-1   Students benefit from the "Read To" program in so many ways—through increased fluency, comprehension, and positive social interactions.

backgrounds and experiences, but traditional tales and favorites were also included as were some informational texts.

As the students bond through careful matching of culture and interests, the benefits are seen in the classroom oral language, reading, and writing programs. There has been a noticeable increase in the younger students' confidence in relating to their peers as well as children of other ages. Teachers have been pleased with the way the young readers are able to focus on details within books and the enthusiasm with which they choose to read and browse through books. The older students have increased their comprehension and fluency as readers and a family feel has developed within the school.

Although the "Read To" program has not focused specifically on informational texts, a number of these books are included in the selection. But, more importantly, the young readers have many opportunities to increase their knowledge about the world and to acquire language to describe it and their unique experiences. The students' newly found curiosity in the world around them provides a solid foundation for success and enjoyment as they begin instruction through the guided reading of informational texts in a supportive atmosphere with their buddy readers.

PART 4

Guided Writing: A Support System for Informational Writing

Authors of chapters in this section make a plea for guided writing to receive as much attention as guided reading. Much of the assessment across curriculum subjects is done through writing—especially the writing of reports or summaries. In order for students to be able to devote their efforts on the content of their writing, they need to be familiar with the structure and features of the various writing forms of informational texts. The forms that are read during guided reading establish the foundation for the intentional teaching provided in guided writing lessons. The adage of "only being able to get from the bank that which has been put in" is true for writing from reading. Teachers who have implemented guided writing sessions have found that the guided writing lessons provide relevant and worthwhile applications of skills and strategies acquired through reading, increasing their students' "residue of learning."

17
Guided Writing

MARGARET MOONEY

Many teachers have realized the benefits of tailoring instruction through guided reading to extend the competence and confidence of small groups of students. However, *guided writing*, which affords the same potential for intentional teaching and focused learning, does not seem to receive the same attention or be an essential part of some literacy programs. Yet students' development as writers as well as readers can be greatly enhanced by receiving instruction of specific skills and strategies of increasing complexity through the guided approach—and especially when the focus is on informational texts with strong visuals.

A Typical Guided Writing Lesson

Six or eight children are seated at a table, their books, pens, spelling and word resources (for example, alphabet cards, blend cards, personal dictionaries, prompt cards) at the ready. The lesson begins with an introductory discussion about the topic, form, skill, or technique that is the instructional focus of the lesson. In most cases, only one or two of these elements would be stressed to allow in-depth instruction while leaving some choice for the students. The teacher would then explicitly demonstrate the composition of a piece, talking through the thinking, decisions, and revisions as the piece is developed.

Depending on the level of the students, three or four key elements to be included in their writing would be identified. This provides a framework to assist the students in the planning, writing, and assessing of their work. Sometimes these two steps are reversed, with the teacher using the criteria as an assessment rubric of her writing. Designing a framework before the lesson means the students not only know their goals and the focus of the assessment, but they have a prompt or schema to help them keep on track, sustain effort, and develop an identifiable shape in their writing.

The students are encouraged to spend time planning their writing, sharing their ideas, and also sharing the first sentence or so with the teacher before putting pen to paper. This enables the teacher to check that the new skill or focus is understood and the framework is firmly in place to sustain each student through the writing. Each student begins writing as soon as the brief discussion with the teacher has concluded. The group members are then working at their individual paces, enabling the teacher to circulate among the students and provide guidance on or answer questions on the application of:

- skills or techniques currently being emphasized
- use of resources for accuracy and alternative words
- pencil hold and letter formation
- layout
- appropriate visual features
- strategies for revision and editing

- maintaining the flow of meaning through rereading and referring to the rubric or framework
- assessment throughout the writing

The focus is on assisting each student achieve the best possible writing through extending their repertoire of skills and application and working toward accurate and fluent writing without detracting from their flow of thought. The guided approach encourages some revision and editing throughout, enabling more focused work on these parts of the process once the draft has been completed. The teacher is able to spend a few minutes talking with each student about their writing, the effort they applied, and how the criteria helped frame and support the writing.

The benefits of guided writing include:

- continuous conferencing between teacher and student and among students
- instruction of appropriate level and intensity for each student
- sustaining on-task focus and effort
- establishing habits to be applied when working in a larger group or independently
- ensuring writing receives the same depth of instruction and value of attention as that given to reading
- providing immediate feedback and establishing new goals

Working with a small group also allows the teacher to be very specific about the similarities and differences between reading and writing and between writing fictional and informational texts. For example:

- The main purpose of fiction is to entertain or to transport readers into another situation. The final scenes are very much as the writer thinks or sees characters and events. In informational texts, the writing reflects what the writer knows or can explain and justify with key information.

Figure 17-1   Guided writing groups ensure that writing receives the same depth of instruction and value of attention as that given to reading.

- The theme or plot shapes a piece of fiction. The writer of informational text focuses on a topic and the implications of elements, change, or interaction with other elements or objects, often requiring research or more detailed planning about what to include before writing begins.

- Most fiction is written in sequence, whereas some informational text can be written in discrete sections, reorganized at the revision stage.

- Visual elements of informational texts are part of the actual composition and not an adjunct added once writing has been completed; or, as in the case of some beginning writers, illustrations completed before the text is written.

In process writing we have become used to whole-class mini-lessons followed by intensive supports at the assessment stage of the final product. Guided writing provides small-group guidance during drafting to support the entire process more effectively.

Guided writing keeps the focus on the "how" of writing at all stages of the process, ensuring the "what" is as the writer intended and is clear to the reader.

18

Linking Guided Reading and Guided Writing

LINDA HOYT

We know that children learn more when learning moments are linked together, when there is a unified focus that draws different elements of the day into a unified whole. Sometimes, that focus might be a theme that unifies science or social studies concepts and becomes the focus of reading, writing, and oral language development. Sometimes, the focus is a strategy such as visualizing that can be applied in math, science, social studies, reading, and writing. The important issue is creating links to support learner understanding and to increase the likelihood that the strategies and content will be remembered and applied in many contexts.

As teachers have worked to become proficient in providing guided reading instruction, there are situations in which learners are having little opportunity to write about what they read or to use their reading as models for writing. We know that when learners write about what they read, they remember more (Pearson 2000). Literacy centers, seatwork activities that are self-contained, and brief interactions have become commonplace activities during the language arts block as teachers try to free themselves for guided reading instruction. However, the activities can become an end in themselves with little connection to building proficiency in the forms of writing that are so richly displayed during guided reading. The concern felt by many is that if centers and seatwork activities are not linked to core content or the instructional focus of the guided reading lesson, we have lost important links in learning, and most certainly lost significant amounts of writing time.

When guided reading and guided writing are linked, students have more opportunity to learn content as they explore it outside of the guided reading group. They have more opportunity to understand the language and text features they encountered in reading if they attempt to utilize those forms in their own writing.

Linkages between guided reading and guided writing can result in a pattern where a guided reading group might read one day and discuss their writing on the same topic the next day. It might result in a community sharing session at the end of language arts where students meet and talk about the writing projects they engaged in as a follow-up to their guided reading experiences. Or, guided writing may occur during the writers workshop time where linkage is focused on connecting the guided writing lesson with individual writing projects.

The following lessons are designed to showcase some possibilities for strengthening the connections between guided reading and guided writing. Their purpose is to affirm your current practices, offer insights into familiar practices, and to stimulate your thinking about strengthening the links across the various areas of your curriculum.

Links to Text Forms, Features, and Organizational Patterns

Sample #1:
Guided Reading Focus: Diagrams in Informational Text

In a text such as *What's Living at Your Place?* by Bruce Chapman, focus your guided reading group on the wide array of diagrams the author has used to communicate information about animals and insects that make their homes in our homes and our yards. Engage the students in a discussion about the role of diagrams. How did the diagrams help them better understand the animals and insects in the book? Did the diagrams cause them to notice parts on the bodies of the insects they might not have noticed in an unlabled photograph?

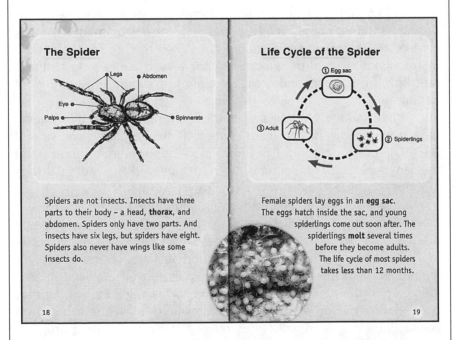

Figure 18-1   The diagrams from page 18 in What's Living at Your Place? *by Bruce Chapman (Pacific Learning), offers strong support to the text on the page and greatly expands the information base for the reader.*

(Continues)

Links to Text Forms, . . . *(Continued)*

Guided Writing Focus: Diagrams in Informational Text

A guided writing experience to link to the guided reading session in sample #1 could focus learners on using diagrams as tools in their writing. Using content from their guided reading selection or content area studies, writers could consider which type of diagram would best suit the writing they are planning. In this small, supported setting they could consider the purpose and audience for their writing and plan how their message could be communicated through text and a diagram. The goal would be to help writers assimilate diagrams into their writers toolbox.

Sample # 1 © 2003 by Linda Hoyt, Margaret Mooney, and Brenda Parkes from *Exploring Informational Texts*. Portsmouth, NH: Heinemann. Figure 18-1© by Bruce Chapman, reprinted with permission.

Sample #2:
Guided Reading Focus: Directions

Guide students in exploring the features of directions: the materials list, the list of steps, the introduction, and the purpose. As you explore the various portions of the direction format, engage students in a conversation about the order in which you might read the sections and related actions you might take as you read. Would you read the whole thing at once? Would you use the materials list to gather supplies before following the steps in the direction sequence? Why is there an introduction? Is this important? Students really enjoy the hands-on experience of gathering supplies and actually following the steps in a set of directions. Please see Figure 18–2. (I recently observed in a classroom where the guided reading group was reading a book that provided directions for making several different types of puppets. The children had a wonderful time reading the various directions, identifying similarities and differences in the structure of each set of directions, then voting on which puppets they would actually make as an extension to guided reading. This became even more powerful when the teacher explained their guided writing follow-up.)

Guided Writing Focus: Directions

This group of students was challenged to follow the steps in the directions and actually make one of the puppets. They were then to return the books to their teacher and write a set of directions telling how their puppet was made. They were to include a materials list, a purpose or introduction, and a list of steps in constructing the puppet.

Lastly, photocopies of their directions were made and this group of students was placed on the class schedule to teach the puppet-making process to the entire class. The result was an in-depth knowledge of how directions are structured, a rich language-building opportunity, and a clear linkage between their reading and writing experiences.

(*Continues*)

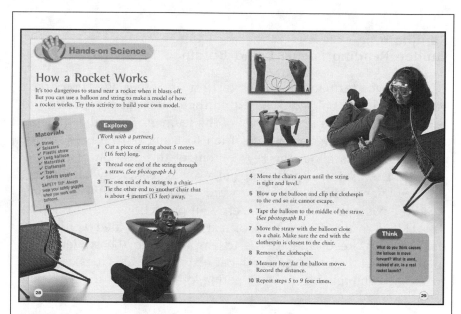

Figure 18-2   Notice the structure of directions: an introduction, list of materials, and list of steps.

Sample # 2 © 2003 by Linda Hoyt, Margaret Mooney, and Brenda Parkes from *Exploring Informational Texts*. Portsmouth, NH: Heinemann. Figure 18-2 © by the National Geographic Society, reprinted with permission.

Sample #3:
Guided Reading Focus: Using Boldface Type

Use a science text, social studies text, or any other age-appropriate text that features boldface type within the context of paragraphs and is appropriate to the reading level of the learners. Show the students how to skim for the bold words. Then focusing on the bold words, make predictions about the key content of this section of reading. Discuss: How can the bold words guide us as readers? What support do they offer a reader? Do these words tend to be in the glossary? Read the passage to see how closely your predictions reflect the passage. Move to the next section of text. Skim for bolded words. Predict. Discuss. Read. The goal is to emphasize to the students the importance of the bold words in most texts. These are clues designed to assist comprehension by targeting our attention to important ideas.

Guided Writing Focus: Using Boldface Words Within Writing

Guide the students in planning a piece of independent or group writing. Explain that their writing will have the purpose of explaining the content in such a way that a younger student could understand. Before they begin writing, they will need to select a few words that they believe are essential to understanding the content. Within their writing, they will highlight these words with bold writing to assist the younger students in grasping the concepts. When the writing is clear and important words written in bold type, the writers are ready to meet with a group of younger children to share their writing and the content they have learned. Page 127 shows an example created by my students:

(Continues)

BABY PENGUINS

When a baby penguin is born it has **down** on its body. Down is a covering of soft feathers which are not waterproof so the baby needs to stay on **land** until it gets bigger feathers.

While the baby waits for adult feathers so it can go swimming, the parents need to bring food to the baby. The mom and dad take turns swimming in the ocean where they catch fish. The mom or dad eats the fish then **regurgitate** it in small bits for the baby to eat.

Sample #4:
Guided Reading Focus: Persuasive Informational Text

Real estate advertisements in the classified section of the newspaper, furniture store advertisements, travel brochures, sales brochures, and many other persuasive forms of informational texts abound in daily life. To focus a guided reading group on persuasive informational texts, you could use such sources from your community or a guided reading sample such as the one below.

Figure 18-3　　Example of persuasive info texts from Pacific Learning

(Continues)

Guided Reading Focus: Persuasive . . . *(Continued)*
What do you notice about persuasive writing? Does it sound like the writing we encounter in a textbook? How is it different? Why? What does the author of this persuasive text want us to know or to do? How does the author try to convince us? Let's compare this piece of persuasive writing to a classified home ad and a letter to the editor I cut from the newspaper. What are the similarities and differences?

Guided Writing Focus: Persuasive Informational Text
Your job is to read several classified ads in the newspaper for homes and businesses that are for sale. Notice the language, sentence length, and layout of the text. Write an advertisement as though you were trying to sell this classroom, this school, or your own home. Try to make your language and format look and sound like a real persuasive ad. Extend students' understanding of persuasive writing with letters to the principal, a newspaper, editor, development of a brochure for visitors to your school, campaign brochures for school elections, and so on.

Sample #5:
Guided Reading Focus: Showing the Passage of Time in Informational Texts

Provide students with an informational text that shows passage of time. This could be a passage that shows a life cycle such as the life cycle of the butterfly, a scientist's journal showing observational logs with dates and times, or a biography that spans time in a human life.

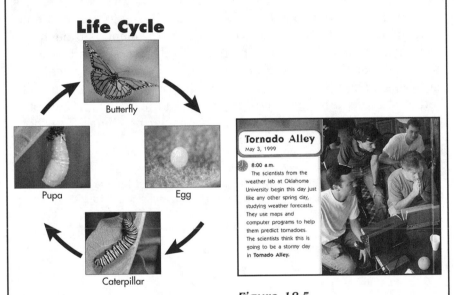

Figure 18-4

Fly Butterfly Fly, by Brenda Parkes (Newbridge Educational)

Figure 18-5

Chasing Tornados! by McGuffy and Burley (Rigby)

Engage the students in sharing observations of how the passage of time was reflected in each of these books. What tools did the writer use in the text and in the visuals? How do these help us understand?

Guided Writing Focus: Passage of Time

Depending on the age of your students, units of study currently in place in your classroom, and interests of the children, guided writing experiences focused on passage of time might include:

- an interactive writing on a day in the classroom, noting times and activity changes
- a daily observational log of the weather, the growth of a seedling, or the maturation of a tadpole in your classroom
- personal autobiographies

The key is to continue to emphasize how we show passage of time. What are our options for expressing time? Which formats fit which purposes? Does a chart communicate needed information?

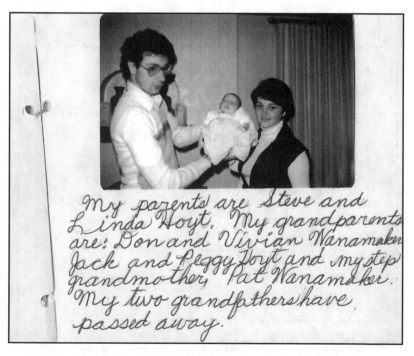

My parents are Steve and Linda Hoyt. My grandparents are: Don and Vivian Wanamaker Jack and Peggy Hoyt and my step grandmother, Pat Wanamaker. My two grandfathers have passed away.

Figure 18-6   An autobiography by Brenden shows passage of time through careful pagination.

(Continues)

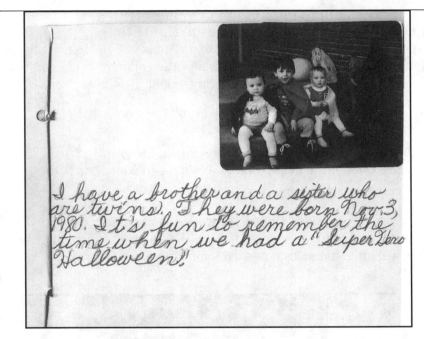

I have a brother and a sister who are twins. They were born Nov. 3, 1980. It's fun to remember the time when we had a "Super Hero Halloween!"

In the future I wish to have lots of friends and for people to respect me for who I am.

Figure 18-6,   Continued

Sample # 5 © 2003 by Linda Hoyt, Margaret Mooney, and Brenda Parkes from *Exploring Informational Texts*. Portsmouth, NH: Heinemann. Figure 18-4 © by Newbridge Educational Publishing, Figure 18-5 © by Rigby, both reprinted with permission.

Sample #6:
Guided Reading Focus: $\boxed{\textit{Preview, Represent, Talk, Read}}$
Teach a guided reading group the strategy of:

$$\boxed{\textit{Preview} \twoheadrightarrow \textit{Represent} \twoheadrightarrow \textit{Talk} \twoheadrightarrow \textit{Read}}$$

as you introduce an informational text. It is important to take take time to really look at the visual features of a page and attempt to comprehend before reading. Preview, Represent, Talk, Read helps readers get the most from a passage. In the following example, a *preview* visual about the Greenhouse Effect offers strong clues as to the content of that passage. Students would *preview* the visual and try to understand what it means. They *represent* it by making a quick sketch or by dramatizing. They then *talk* about what they think is happening. Finally, they *read* and discuss again.

Figure 18-7   Notice how the boldface heading, diagram, and bold text support a prereading discussion.

(Continues)

Preview, Represent, Talk, Read *(Continued)*

It takes time to *preview*, *represent*, and *talk* before reading but it brings tremendous power and understanding to the reading of the passage and results in greater levels of learner understanding.

Guided Writing Focus: $\boxed{Review \rightarrow Represent \rightarrow Talk \rightarrow Write}$

To use this strategy as a writing tool, I ask students to *review* their thinking on a topic of study. They think back to important facts, concepts, and information in the unit or in the reading material. Next they *represent* what they have learned. The third step is to *talk* to their guided writing group about their thinking and the key ideas they represented in their sketch. Lastly, they *write* and share. Review, Represent, Talk, Write brings writing into focus and teaches a process for a generating concise written summaries.

19

Support for Students Writing Informational Texts in Writers Workshop

JERRY A. MILLER

As students become more skilled at writing they naturally want to try their hand at text forms other than personal narrative. Indeed, the proliferation of primary-level nonfiction texts has changed the shape of Writers Workshop by providing budding writers of nonfiction with an array of models. Although nonfiction texts can take many forms, the basic organizational structure of expository writing remains the same: a large topic is split into manageable subtopics, with specific, factual examples and illustrations provided to explain and expand upon the subtopics.

In her book, A *Framework for Understanding Poverty* (1998), Ruby Payne advises giving students "mental models" to assist them in remembering the organizational structure of various text forms. She suggests a hand as a model for expository text, with the topic being represented by the palm and the subtopics represented by the fingers and thumb. Students can easily see the connection between the hand model and the organizational structure of expository writing. They can use the model to help them recall information in texts they read and can use it to plan and organize their own expository writing as well.

The following instructional sequence for introducing the hand model, first in reading, then in writing, has been effective in classrooms across the grade levels:

Introducing the Organizational Structure of Expository Text

Begin by selecting a piece of expository text on a topic of interest to your students.

Draw a large hand on a piece of chart paper.

On the palm, write the topic of the text you have selected, then ask students to predict what subtopics the author will cover. If students have a hard time with the concept of subtopic, just ask them what the different chapters in the book might be about.

Label each of the fingers and the thumb of the hand with a different subtopic.

Select sentences at random from the book and read them aloud to your students. Ask students to identify which "finger" the sentence belongs to.

Demonstrate note-taking by rephrasing the sentence in writing on the appropriate finger of your hand drawing.

The following example came from a discussion with fourth graders predicting the content of a book on the Titanic:

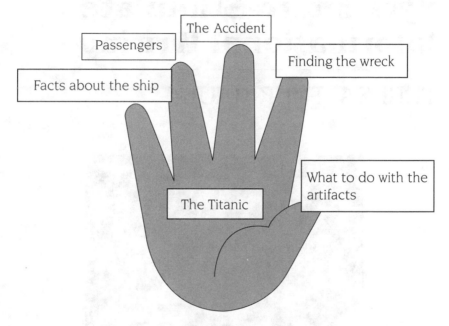

Figure 19-1   Using the model for organizing a piece of expository writing

Once students are familiar with the organizational structure of expository writing, they can use a planning sheet with a hand on it to help them brainstorm ideas for researching and writing. Depending on their level of sophistication, the individual fingers can represent chapters, pages, or paragraphs about the main topic under study.

Of course, not all topics are easily segmented into five subtopics. The hand serves as a model, but not a generic formula that students can use each and every time. They must be encouraged to experiment with the structure once they understand it, so that student expository writing does not become too stilted.

20

Using the Expository Pyramid to Stimulate Informational Writing

TERESA THERRIAULT

Brian Cambourne's *Conditions of Learning* (1988) remind us that engagement is key to successful learning. We know that when students are engaged, their attitude remains positive and they are willing to work to overcome challenges. Often the key to engagement is a supportive framework and, in the case of writing, a schema to help them organize their ideas.

The following pyramid structure adapted from Brenda Waldo's *Story Pyramid* can be used in guided writing to heighten learner awareness of word choice, voice, and organization.

Line 1: Name of animal

Line 2: Two words describing animal

Line 3: Three words describing its habitat

Line 4: Four words describing one of its behaviors

Line 5: Five words describing another behavior

Line 6: Six words describing another behavior

Line 7: Seven words describing another behavior

Line 8: Eight words describing your personal reflections about the animal

Example of Guided Writing Using an adapted Pyramid Structure in Response to Reading About Sloths

Sloth

Timid tree-dweller

Panama's tropical zone

Upside-down toe-hanging wonder

Protective coloration green algae hues

Still canopy life; munching her lunch

Motionless mother gripping firm/being firmly gripped

Marvelous design forest queen perfectly adapted lovely serene

The pyramid helped the writers gather words, phrases and descriptions, As they then considered organization and voice, this pyramid was used to shape the following report.

THE SLOTH

An eerie feeling grips me each time I've stared into the eyes of a sloth. There seems to be an awareness there, beyond mere animal knowledge. It's hard for me to shake the feeling. This amazing creature resides in Panama's tropical zone. She is a timid tree-dweller who rarely leaves her lofty hideaway. Hanging upside-down, clinging with her three-toed grasp, is her life.

She's well adapted to her habitat. Algae grows on her fur from the continuous rain. The algae colors her in shades of green that protect her and her young from predators. Just as the mother sloth clings to the branches of treetops, her baby must . . .

A suggested procedure for implementing the pyramid would begin with the teacher familiarizing herself with the structure, perhaps practicing developing a pyramid and using it as a writing aid. The selection of the book the students will use to gather their information is critical. It must have sufficient detail and description for students to complete the pyramid. The introduction should include a description of the intended outcome and, of course, they will need to see you model the building of a pyramid as you explain your choice of words.

When the students begin to build their own pyramids, it may be appropriate that they work as a team until they have sufficient confidence to do one independently. Further teacher modeling may be necessary as students use the pyramid to develop a piece of connected text. Once the writing has been competed, reflection on the process and the student's self-appraisal of how the framework supported them will reveal new pointers for the next learning opportunities and challenges.

PART 5

Professionals Writing Informational Texts for Young Readers

In this section Brenda Parkes and Margaret Mooney, authors of much-loved books for our young readers, reflect on their thinking as they combine their knowledge of reading development with the goal of communicating information. As you read, enjoy their insights into how their sensitivity to the reader governs their writing.

21

Thinking Behind
the Pen

BRENDA PARKES

Any writing I do for children is based on my current theoretical knowledge about the reading/writing process and what I know about my anticipated audience. My informational books have a dual purpose. On the one hand, they are guided reading books. Therefore I have to carefully consider the balance of supports and challenges I'll provide not only in the language but also in the organizational features, pictures, charts, and diagrams. Each of these have to play an increasingly sophisticated role across emergent, early, and fluent titles. For example, at the emergent level I know I'll mostly be working with one or two lines of print and it will be necessary to build in some repetitive patterns to build confidence and forward momentum. The photos will need to closely match the text as a source of prediction and confirmation. At the fluent level, I have more print to work with and the patterns that support the reader will come more overtly from structural patterns such as cause and effect. By fluent level most of the photos will need to extend the meaning of the text and invite the reader to make inferences.

No matter what reading level is targeted, I need to consider what benchmarks and standards have to be met in either social studies or science and the choices that are available to me to illuminate the concepts in an engaging, meaningful way. It's important to set up the concept at the outset. The covers and title must provide the potential for focused discussion and the first few pages must clearly establish the author's purpose.

Beaks (Parkes 1999) shows how this unfolds at the early level. The front cover photograph of a toucan's head with a huge, open

Figure 21-1   A well designed cover invites the reader into the book, encouraging questions and creating motivation to read.

beak and the back cover photograph of an owl with a small, hooked beak open the way for discussion. They also set up the compare/contrast pattern reflecting how the information is presented in the book.

The written text on page 2 sets the concept in place.

Page 2   Birds have beaks.

Pages 3 and 4 shown here set up the pattern of information.

Figure 21-2   A bird's beak helps it get food and eat it.

This is a parrot. Parrots have short, sharp beaks.

Page 16   This book page shown on the following page as Figure 21-3 asks the readers to summarize and apply what they have been learning.

How is this bird using it's beak?

It is always my hope that my books will provide models and ideas for children's own writing. This is how Joshua used *Beaks* to write and draw about some birds he observed in his neighborhood. See Figure 21-4.

Figure 21-3   *How is this bird using its beak?*

This birds beak is good for fishing.

What kind of food does This bird eat?

Figure 21-4   Notice how this young writer used the pattern of the guided reading selection to organize his own writing.

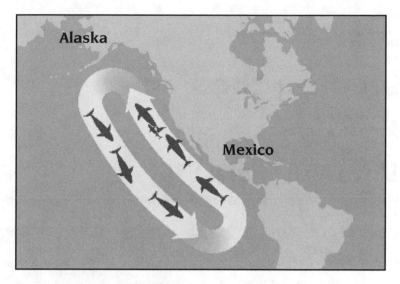

Figure 21-5   Before the winter comes, the whales travel, or migrate, to warmer oceans. The arrows on this map show one migration route. Each summer these whales live in the cold waters near Alaska. Each winter they travel south to live in the warm waters near Mexico.

Understanding and using the information in maps and diagrams is an important skill for content area reading and my book, Watching Whales (Parkes 1999), provided a perfect opportunity for me to combine a map and diagram to illustrate the whales' migratory pattern. This page is set up to help readers conceptualize the whales' annual journey between their breeding and feeding grounds.

It is vitally important that readers learn to integrate information from multiple sources. Research consistently shows that many readers read the written text and ignore maps and diagrams, or look at the maps and diagrams and read the written text but fail to realize they are designed to work together. This single page demonstrates how the pieces work together. It also allows readers to choose where to start their reading and thinking, another feature of informational texts.

Students can read and view this page and through discussion share their interpretation of each piece, how it connects to the others, and how all combine to communicate the information.

22

Keeping the Pen Sharp

MARGARET MOONEY

"Behind the pen" is certainly an appropriate phrase to use when thinking about writing informational texts. Every fact that finds its way onto the page in good informational writing represents hours of research, either through actual experience or through dialogue, reading, and thinking. Any and every detail within each fact has been checked and rechecked. It is often the minutest piece of information that causes readers to discredit or trust an author's work—and especially when the readers are children! None of the forty or so books

I have published has brought this fact home to me more so than *A Matter of Balance* (SRA, 1994). This book has engendered more letters from readers than any of the other books—and almost all of the correspondence has been about details.

> "You wrote that it (the crossing) took eighteen minutes. I read that it took seventeen and a half minutes. Which is right?"
>
> "How did you know how many people watched him cross?"
>
> "What was the manager's name? Why didn't you tell us that?"
>
> "How did he carry the stove onto the tightrope?"
>
> "What would have happened it the stove had burnt the rope?"

Fortunately, the hours I had spent researching and cross-checking every part of each episode before I put pen to paper enabled me to respond in detail to the many correspondents, with the exception of the query about burning the rope. The number and nature of the letters is a constant reminder to me that young readers of informational text are very discerning and that even the smallest inaccuracy could cause them to lose faith in the act of reading.

My experience with *A Matter of Balance* was a reminder that the writer of a good informational text makes it appear to the readers that they have the same camera or set of eyes as the author. The author may have greater powers of magnification, pointing out details the reader has not previously noticed, but the introduction must avoid any hint of condescension resulting in the reader feeling less than adequate. Condescension is to be avoided in any text, but especially in informational texts, and even more so in those for young readers. The learning should come from the two-way dialogue and not from the author shouting in the reader's ear.

I believe an underlying principle of guided reading is that the support we provide during the first half of the reading of a book should build sufficient confidence and competence for the reader to complete the reading with an ever-decreasing amount of guidance. This was certainly an influence behind the pen of *The Busy Harvest* (Newbridge, 2000).

The Busy Harvest   **Contents**
by Margaret Mooney

The first two chapters establish a pattern in the structure of the text, although there are some differences in sentence structure.

FLOWER FARM

It is time for a busy harvest.
The flowers on this farm
are ready to be picked.

Workers pick the flowers
that grow in rows.

This worker puts the flowers
into boxes.

A truck takes the flowers
to markets in the city.

WHEAT FARM

The wheat on this farm
is ready to be cut.
A harvester cuts the wheat.

The harvester sorts the wheat, too.

The grains of wheat are pumped
into a truck.

Then the wheat is taken to big silos.
The wheat is stored in the silos
until it is needed.

The third chapter extends the structure, providing more detailed information.

APPLE ORCHARD

The apples in this orchard
are ready to be picked.

Workers pick the apples.
This worker stands on a ladder
to reach apples
at the tops of trees.

The apples are put into large crates.
A tractor pulls the crates to a shed.

There are different kinds of apples.
The apples are sorted.

Some apples are made into apple juice.
Trucks take the other apples
to stores in the city.

Figure 22-1   Informational texts provide models and motivation for informational writing.

The final page introduces another type of harvest, leaving the reader to write the text in their head using the framework of the previous three harvests.

> Look at these big pumpkins!
> It is time for another busy harvest.

My overriding focus when writing for children is that they learn to trust the acts of reading, discover that informational texts can open doors for continued thought, provide models and motivation for the readers to pick up the pen themselves, and offer the gift of new ideas and knowledge. I want my readers to talk to me, but I know I can only initiate dialogue through the words on the page—so each one has to contribute to the whole. Once the words are printed, my work is done and I have to then trust my readers to continue that dialogue through the words and illustrations. I hope that every word I write will be the springboard for thousands more in a child's head. What a privilege and what a responsibility!

PART 6

Checking Up

I f guided reading of informational texts is as important as the contributors in this book have implicitly and overtly claimed, the reader
of this book could well expect this section to be the longest rather
than the shortest. Assessment is important. It is so important that it
is the foundation and provides a continuous guideline for every
guided reading and writing session. The forms of assessment include
after-chapter tests or reviews, reading of specially selected and previously unseen texts and vocabulary lists, lists of questions to be
answered correctly, and other assessments designed primarily to
assign marks or determine progress in a quantifiable way. But guided
reading is an assessment approach in itself. It is responsive and
responsible teaching, with the teacher in a monitoring and assessing
mode from the moment she begins to plan the first lesson of the year
through the last lesson.

23

Taking Stock of Our Practices

LINDA HOYT

My goal is for readers to be proficient and strategic, to be empowered with tools that will guide them to success in any text they encounter. I want them to be comprehenders who are never satisfied with just *saying words*.

To move closer to that goal, I must consciously challenge my own teaching practices, take careful stock of how I am using time, and wonder if I am teaching strategies or just engaging students in activities.

Time with Text

We must take seriously the time with text issues. Many studies have conclusively proven that there is a direct correlation between time spent reading and performance on standardized measures (Fountas and Pinnell 2001; Allington 2000). It is a simple truth that if you want to be better at reading, you need to read a lot! Just as improvement in skateboarding, golfing, ice skating, or waterskiing requires that you spend time practicing.

Unfortunately, many studies also show that students are spending more time doing follow-up activities than reading (Allington 2000; Calkins 1998). They spend more time listening to the teacher talking than reading. They spend more time answering questions at the end of chapters than they spend reading the content.

As we narrow our view to look closely at informational texts and the role they play in instruction as well as the lifelong literacy needs of our learners, the following questions may be of critical importance:

Are the students spending enough time reading informational texts?

Are they really getting the practice they need to become proficient with these sources?

How are we using class time? Is teacher talk taking more time than student reading? Is guided reading filled with students *reading*?

Are activities or worksheets taking more time than the reading itself?

Are all students, even those reading below grade level, having extensive time to read info sources at their just-right level?

Are students receiving small-group support as writers of informational texts?

Unfortunately, I see many students, especially those who are below-grade-level readers, getting through entire days with very small amounts of reading. These students are often short-stopped by a more proficient reader who skims quickly and comes up with an answer before the first child even finishes reading. These students are often the ones who *listen* while others read. It is critical that teachers reflect on time with text if we hope to bring all learners to their highest levels of potential.

Teaching Reading Strategies for Extracting Meaning

There was a time when I provided students with a wide array of worksheets and activities because I thought they were helping them learn the content. These activities also freed me to work with individuals or small groups. I now stand back and wonder about the activities I choose. With each one I ask, "Is this teaching a strategic behavior the student can utilize in another book or is this only helpful with this one book or this one unit of study?" If the answer is, "just this book or unit," then I need to step back and wonder . . .

What strategy *could* I teach that will deepen understanding *and* be a tool for the learner to carry into other books?

Key Questions

Am I teaching the students strategies they can use in many texts?

What will happen if I have students read more and practice strategies?

Will they really be reading? Will they like it? Will they learn the content?

If I don't do the worksheet or the questions at the end of the chapter, will I be missing important content?

Which strategies might best benefit my students?

Do they have an array of tools for extracting meaning from informational texts?

What strategies do I use when I read for information?
Would the students benefit from learning some of my personal strategies?

I want to focus on teaching strategies that students can put in their pocket and carry away to the books they will read tomorrow, next week, and in several years. These strategies need to support extraction of information, be flexible and easy to use, and generalize across many texts and content areas.

The following email from Raymond Iacovone of New Jersey mirrors this focus and why it is so important.

Dear Mrs. Hoyt,

I just wanted to thank you for a wonderful seminar yesterday!

I tried an "experiment" today that really proved your point for me. In the morning, I followed my lesson plans exactly as I had written them. I noted the students reading time, which turned out to be *less than five minutes*.

Right before lunch, we threw out the lesson plans and covered "what makes a good reader" (abridged for fifth graders).

After lunch, I presented shorter lessons that focused on reading strategies rather than content. We covered Read, Cover, Remember, and Retell; and Keywording in three different subject areas. What a difference!

Students spent over one hour READING and that included one half hour in a science lab activity. I now have posters around the room to remind students of what makes a good reader and the reading strategies we have learned. I'm sure I will be asking students to identify which strategy they use very soon.

Another by-product of students spending more time reading was improved discipline in the class. What a pleasant surprise! I am sold on your approach to spending more time reading.

My lesson plans and actual lessons will look much different from now on.

Congratulations on making a convert.

Sincerely,
Raymond Iacovone
Newfield, New Jersey

P.S. I know I might have missed a step or two in explaining what happened today. Please excuse any oversights due to my excitement. Thanks again.

(See *Revisit, Reflect, Retell*, Hoyt 1999, for information on Read, Cover, Remember, Retell.)

Teaching an Array of Meaning-Seeking Strategies

I believe that it is important for students to have a tool belt that is laden with the strategies listed on the following page *and* an array of strategies that are designed to extract the big ideas and supporting details from text. I consciously teach a variety of these meaning-seeking strategies as every strategy doesn't work for every text. I often listen to students debriefing a reading session with comments such as:

> I started with the Key Word Strategy and it just wasn't working for me. I checked the strategy list on the wall and decided to use the VIP strategy instead. In this book, it just seemed to work a little better.

As you consider various strategies for informational texts, please keep in mind that all will need to be modeled several times.

Good Reader Strategies

Good Readers:

- Have clear goals for their reading
- Look over the text before reading
- Activate prior knowledge
- Make predictions
- Use meaning and expect the text to make sense
- Understand whether or not comprehension is occurring
- Make connections: text to self, text to text, text to world
- Create visual images
- Use text features (pictures, headings, boldface type)
- Draw inferences and conclusions
- Ask questions as they read
- Make inferences and draw conclusions
- Read different kinds of texts, differently
    - √ In narrative, attend to characters and plot
    - √ In expository, construct and revise summaries skim and scan to recheck information can locate information
    - √ Adjust rate to match the demands of the text
- Identify important ideas and words
- Consciously shift strategies
- Retell, summarize, synthesize
- Use a variety of fix-up strategies
    - √ Read on
    - √ Backtrack
    - √ Context clues
    - √ Make substitutions
    - √ Look at word parts: beginnings, endings, chunks

Figure 23-1   Modeling and feedback are vital support systems as learners attempt to apply effective reading strategies.

In Raymond's email, he mentioned modeling one strategy in three different content areas. Modeling is a key factor in helping students internalize these meaning-seeking strategies.

24

Some Assessment Tools

CHERYLE FERLITA

Rubric for Assessing the Summarizing of Informational Text

The following rubric is not designed to assign grades but is used as a tool for identifying teaching points for subsequent guided reading sessions. A student may be excellent in one area of the rubric, but just beginning in another area—this is normal so teachers need to be careful not to confine their assessment to any one section. When

RUBRIC

Excellent

The student demonstrates a complete understanding of the text through discussion.

The student summarizes the text in a logical sequence.

The student consistently uses information and details from the text to support the text summary.

The student states the topic of the text in the summary.

The student includes the most important information or main ideas and omits information that is irrelevant to the topic.

The student consistently identifies the author's purpose.

The student can provide information from the text to support the author's purpose.

The student can provide information about the connection between the visual supports and the main body of the text.

Learning

The student demonstrates a partial understanding of the text.

The student summarizes the text using mostly relevant information but some minor concepts are included.

The student usually locates details or information from the text to support their summary.

The student states ideas as topics during the summary or refers to the topic with referent words only.

The student includes most of the key information but refers to some information that is irrelevant to the summary.

The student states the author's purpose but is unable to support this purpose with evidence from the text.

The student can explain the visuals but is unsure of how they support the text.

(Continues)

RUBRIC *(Continued)*

More Focus Needed

The student demonstrates a limited understanding of the information in the text.

The student lists information from the text including relevant and minor details.

The student states a detail from the text when asked about the author's purpose.

The student is aware of the visual supports in the text, but is unsure how they fit or what they mean.

The student needs to be prompted with many inquiry questions during the summary.

Beginning

The student demonstrates a minimal level of understanding of the text.

The student's summary is unorganized and includes information from the text in a random fashion.

The student is unsure of the topic or any of the main ideas of the text.

The student does not discuss the author's purpose or give a purpose of the text even when prompted.

The student does not read, understand, or see the relevance of the visual supports in the text.

assessing students' ability to summarize informational text, I feel they should be able to discuss the main idea of the text, discuss the author's purpose and point of view, show they understand the role of visual supports, and demonstrate in their discussion a complete understanding of the text.

Reading Conference for Information Text

The student brings an informational book to the conference. It should be a book that is currently being read. Or, the teacher selects several titles and the student chooses one. If the book is familiar the conference can proceed but if the text is unseen, the student should have time to become familiar with the topic and gain some idea of how it is presented. The teacher is careful to record behaviors and observations as the student reads.

READING CONFERENCE FORM

Reading behaviors _____
_____
_____
_____
_____
_____
_____
_____

Tell me about what you just read. _____
_____
_____
_____
_____
_____
_____

If the student has difficulty getting started, use some of the following prompts:

> What is the topic of the book?
>
> How does the author present the information?
>
> Why did the author write this?
>
> What were some of the important points in the text?
>
> What did you learn from reading this?
>
> What did you learn about the topic that you did not already know?

Were there parts of the book that you did not understand? What questions do you still have? What puzzled you? _____
_____
_____
_____
_____
_____

(Continues)

How did the author organize or arrange the text? Do you see a pattern or something the author used over and over? _____

_____

_____

_____

Show me a place where you figured out a word because of clues the author gave you. _____

_____

_____

What would you like to see the author add to this text? _____

_____

_____

_____

What viewpoint does the author take on this topic? Is anyone else's opinion presented? _____

_____

_____

_____

How long do you think it will take you to finish this text? _____

_____

_____

_____

What subjects would you like to read about next? _____

_____

_____

How do you decide what to read about? _____

_____

_____

_____

Figure 24-1   *Reading Conference Form*

25

Assessment Through Application

NORMA GIBBS

The best assessment of the long-term benefits of learning is the way in which strategies and knowledge are applied in a range of real-life situations. The staff of Mangere Bridge Elementary School, a multi-cultural school of 450 students in Auckland, New Zealand, work hard to create opportunities within the school that require the children to transfer and extend their learning beyond the context of the reading and writing period. Two such opportunities focusing on applying learning about informational texts are the school bank and the involvement of students learning English as a second language in the management of the school library.

The banking service is linked to one of the national commercial banks, working as an offshoot of the local branch. Students in years 5 and 6 are trained by staff from the local bank, but work under the supervision of the school principal when the bank opens before school one morning each week. Students and parents are able to deposit money with the student-bankers. They have full responsibility for manually recording all transactions in the bank ledger and client's bankbooks. Courteous service, safe handling of money, and accuracy of recording are key to the continuous running of the school bank. Students throughout the school are becoming familiar with one aspect of the importance of informational texts within the context of daily life.

The following case study, also from Mangere Bridge School, relates more specifically to students learning English who are applying their learning about informational text in another real-life situation. English as a Second Language Tutor and Library Assistant Pauline Kumar views the library as a "user-friendly" place where you do not have to be a fluent reader or speaker of the English language to enjoy a book, play a game, or use the technical equipment available to everyone. This supports the school's belief that the library is the heart of the school and should be a center of learning for all students, teachers, parents, and the wider school community including preschoolers.

Pauline viewed her librarian skills as a way to enhance the English language learning of her English language learners through the development of a program that would not only continue to train the upper-grade students as librarians, but extend it to those students she worked with as a language tutor. During the planning stages of this library project, Pauline considered the students' strong desire to be part of the dominant language group and the preference some of the students showed for informational rather than fictional text. Her knowledge of the culturally diverse students and of the learning styles, values, and customs of those cultures influenced the material she selected and her decision to work with a small group of students. She knew that the cooperative learning style of students from the Pacific Islands (with their concept of the extended family and ability to relate to all age groups) could be utilized effectively in the proposed project while also suiting the students of Asian and Chinese backgrounds.

All lessons helping the students become proficient users of the library and assistants in its management have followed the same format, although there have been some refinement for specific groups or individual students. In the first group, three students used English fluently and three spoke English as their second or other language. Pauline was anxious to train all as librarians but also hoped that increasing their personal use of the library would also support the developing literacy skills of the three students learning English. The group lesson began with a focus on getting to know each other, familiarizing the students with their goals, exploring the picture book section of the library, and interacting with each other. Pauline was careful that the students who spoke and read English fluently provided good models and she paid attention to communicating content knowledge as more than word-by-word decoding. The next two lessons involved having the students find puzzles, word games, and listening tapes available in the library and sharing these with each other. This quickly instilled a feeling of confidence and helped the new students familiarize themselves with the library.

From this point, the lessons each day began with the review of a favorite book, game, or puzzle and of skills learned in previous lessons. Interactions between the students became more relaxed and lively. The students began to use the library telephone to answer calls and exchange messages. Lessons focusing on the skills necessary to be a library assistant then began in earnest. These included learning how to operate the computer program, how to use the scanner for check-in and check-out, shelving returned or new picture, fiction, and nonfiction books, and where to locate parent or teacher resources. The students were encouraged to take home books written in their predominant language to share with their family. They were encouraged to invite their parents to the library to see what was available to the family as well as to show off their newly acquired skills as a library assistant. Books in two languages were shared among the group and the students also shared these in their classrooms.

After two weeks of daily lessons, the students were full-fledged librarians who carried out library duty at lunchtime when the library was open for all students. They learned about a duty roster and received further training in communicating with students of all ages. Their confidence and ability in spoken English increased noticeably as did their reading and library skills. They learned how to access topic-specific material, use tables of content and indexes, and apply dictionary skills quickly and accurately. All members of the group have opted to complete the goals required to receive a bronze, silver, and gold Librarians Awards.

Librarian Awards

Bronze

Scan books for issue

Stamp book in correct place

Scan books returned

Tidy all bookshelves, spines facing outward

Shelve fiction and picture books correctly

Choose books for face-out display

Silver

Glue issue slip in correctly

Label book spines

Use computer to locate books using "fast find"

Shelve nonfiction books correctly using Dewey system

Check shelves for books in need of repair

Gold

Use the index of an encyclopedia to locate information

Use computer to search using keywords and NASH book

Complete and Accessit book review

Write about the author of the book reviewed

Pauline and the staff of Mangere Bridge School are heartened by the success of the library project and are continuing the project. The students have become accomplished library assistants, respected by their peers, confident in themselves, and competent applying their learning in real-life situations.

Contributors

Kathy Baird, McMinnville, Oregon
Kathy has taught primary grades for many years, served as a Reading Recovery Teacher Leader, and is currently a staff developer for McMinnville School District in Oregon. Her passion for children and teaching has also led her into photography. Kathy took the photos that grace the back cover of this book, the front matter, and many of the interior pages.

Janine Batzle, Irvine, California
Janine Batzle is a national literacy consultant and author. She has developed video programs, *Guided Reading: The Child Centered Classroom* and *Creating and Managing the Child Centered Classroom* (Rigby, 1996), as well as the publications *Portfolio Assessment* (1992), *The Bridge to Written Language: Phonemic Awareness* (2001), and *Best Practice: Guided Reading*, a position paper (2002). Currently, she is field-testing *Assessment to Instruction*, a research-based comprehension assessment system. Ms. Batzle works with teachers in ongoing professional development and is completing her doctoral program at USC in educational administration.

Nell K. Duke, Michigan State University
Nell K. Duke is an assistant professor at Michigan
State University. Her award-winning research,
conducted independently and through CIERA, has
provided important guidance in reading comprehension instruction, early literacy development
among children living in poverty, as well as the
development of informational literacies.

Cheryle Ferlita, Tampa, Florida
Cheryle Ferlita has spent many years teaching in a
variety of settings including elementary, secondary,
and special education. She is currently serving at
the district level as a staff development specialist
in the area of reading.

Norma Gibbs, Auckland, New Zealand
Norma Gibbs is a teacher/administrator from a
large multicultural school in Auckland,
New Zealand. She has taught extensively in
New Zealand and is primarily interested in the
acquisition of literacy and numeracy in the first
three years of school.

Linda Hoyt, Sherwood, Oregon
Linda Hoyt is the author of *Revisit, Reflect, Retell:
Strategies for Improving Reading Comprehension*
(Heinemann, 1999); *Snapshots: Literacy Minilessons Up
Close* (Heinemann, 2000), and *Make It Real: Strategies
for Success with Informational Texts* (Heinemann, 2002)
as well as an array of video programs. Linda is a
reading specialist with thirty years of experience
in elementary schools and teacher education
programs.

Jan McCall, Beaverton, Oregon
Jan McCall has taught for many years in elementary classrooms where her combined love of children and reading has provided impetus for powerful innovations in literacy education. She currently works as a reading specialist and Title I Literacy Facilitator in Beaverton, Oregon.

Jerry A. Miller, Issaquah, Washington
Jerry Miller is with the Issaquah School District where he combines classroom teaching with facilitating teacher development. He is the author of the foreword for Margaret Mooney's *Text Forms and Features* and a teacher who clearly shows passion for quality teaching and self-reflective practice.

Margaret Mooney, Auckland, New Zealand
Margaret Mooney has written many books for young readers and resource books for teachers, including her most recent, *Text Forms and Features: A Resource for Intentional Teaching* (Richard C. Owen, 2000). She spent twenty years as a teacher and administrator in New Zealand elementary schools, with special emphasis on the first three years of schooling. She worked with the New Zealand Department of Education and at the university level. In 1988 Margaret was awarded the Order of New Zealand Merit by Queen Elizabeth II for her work in literacy.

Michael F. Opitz, Manitou Springs, Colorado
Former elementary school teacher and reading specialist, Dr. Michael F. Opitz is a professor of reading education at the University of Northern Colorado. He is the author of seven books including *Reaching Readers: Flexible and Innovative Strategies for Guided Reading* (Heinemann, 2001), *Rhymes and Reasons: Literature and Language Play for Phonological Awareness* (Heinemann, 2000), *Good-Bye Round Robin* (Heinemann, 1998), *Flexible Grouping in Reading*

(Scholastic, 1998), and *Literacy Instruction for Culturally and Linguistically Diverse Students* (International
Reading Association, 1998). He is also an author
of *Summer Success Reading* (Great Source, 2001), a
reading program designed to help children who
need additional help with reading. Michael's
articles appear in professional and trade journals

Brenda Parkes, Melbourne, Australia
Dr. Parkes has written many books for children
including *Who's in the Shed? The Enormous Watermelon,
Goodnight, Goodnight and the Runaway Pizza*. She has
taught in New Zealand and Australia and spent
twenty years as a teacher educator at Griffith
University, Queensland. Her most recent professional book is *Read It Again: Revisiting Shared Reading*
(Stenhouse, 2000).

Teresa Therriault, San Diego, California
Teresa Therriault has been involved in education for
nearly thirty years working in special needs, as a
classroom teacher, with talented and gifted programs,
and Title I. She has worked as a district-level literacy
facilitator as a District Language Arts Specialist.
Teresa and her husband live in San Diego where she
works as an independent literacy consultant.

Jodi Wilson, Couer d'Alene, Idaho
Jodi Wilson has experienced many different career
opportunities in education. She has worked as a
classroom teacher, national literacy consultant,
mentor, early childhood facilitator, staff developer,
reading specialist, and author. With each new bend
and twist in her educational journey, Jodi has
always thrived on the new challenges presented by
the teaching and learning process. Jodi currently
works for the Spokane School District in Spokane,
Washington as an Early Childhood
Facilitator/Mentor.

Bibliography and References

Allington, R. 2001. *What Really Matters for Struggling Students: Designing Research-Based Programs.* New York: Longman

Anderson, E., and J. T. Guthrie. 1999, April. *Motivating Children to Gain Conceptual Knowledge from Text: The Combination of Science Observation and Interesting Texts.* Paper presented at the Annual Meeting of the American Educational Research Association, Montreal, CA.

Armstrong, J. O., M. Wise, C. Janisch, and L. A. Meyer 1991. "Reading and Questioning in Content Area Lessons." *Journal of Reading Behavior* 23.

Atwell, N. ed. 1990. *Coming to Know: Writing to Learn in the Intermediate Grades.* Portsmouth, NH: Heinemann.

Bamford, R. A., and J. V. Kristo, eds. 1998. *Making Facts Come Alive: Choosing Quality Nonfiction Literature K–12.* Norwood, MA: Christopher Gordon.

Bamford, R. A., and J. V. Kristo, eds. 2000. *Checking Out Nonfiction K–8: Good Choices for Best Learning.* Norwood, MA: Christopher Gordon.

Block, C. C., and M. Pressley, eds. 2002. *Comprehension Instruction: Research-Based Best Practices.* New York: The Guilford Press.

Bridges, L. 1997. *Writing as a Way of Knowing.* York, ME: Stenhouse Publishers.

Buehl, D. 2001. *Classroom Strategies for Interactive Learning.* Newark, DE: International Reading Association.

Caswell, L. J., and N. K. Duke. 1998. "Non-narrative as a Catalyst for Literacy Development." *Language Arts* 75: 108–117.

Cerullo, M. M. 1997. *Reading the Environment: Children's Literature in the Science Classroom.* Portsmouth, NH: Heinemann.

Chall, J. S. 1983. *Stages of Reading Development.* New York: McGraw-Hill.

Clay, M. 1991. *Becoming Literate: The Construction of Inner Control.* Portsmouth, NH: Heinemann.

Creenaune, T., and L. Rowles. 1996. *What's Your Purpose? Reading Strategies for Nonfiction Texts.* Sydney, Australia: Primary English Teachers Association.

Cruz, P. C. 2000. *Guided Reading: Making it Work.* Jefferson County, MO: Scholastic Professional Books.

Cunningham, D., D., and S. C. Hall. 1998. *The Teacher's Guide to the Four Blocks.* Greensboro, NC: Carson-Dellosa.

Department of Education, Western Australia. 1995. *First Steps.* Portsmouth, NH: Heinemann

Derewianka, B. 1990. *Exploring How Texts Work.* Sydney, Australia: Primary English Teaching Association.

Donovan, C., and L. Smolkin. 2002. "Considering Genre, Content, and Visual Features in the Selection of Trade Books for Science Instruction." *The Reading Teacher* 55 (6): 502–519.

Donovan, C. A., and L. B. Smolkin. 2001. "Genre and Other Factors Influencing Teachers' Book Selection for Science Instruction." *Reading Research Quarterly* 36 (4): 412–440.

Dreher, M. J. 2000. "Fostering Reading for Learning." In *Engaging Young Readers: Promoting Achievement and Motivation* edited by L. Baker, M. J. Dreher, and J. Guthrie, pp. 94–118. New York: Guilford.

Dreher, M. J. 2002. "Children Searching and Using Informational Text." In *Comprehension Instruction: Research-Based Best Practices*, edited by Cathy Collins Block and Michael Pressley, 289–304. New York: The Guilford Press.

Duke, N. K. 2000. "3–6 Minutes per Day: The Scarcity of Informational Texts in First Grade." *Reading Research Quarterly* 35 (2): 202–224.

Duke, N. K. 2002. *Reading to Learn from the Very Beginning: Informational Literacy in Early Childhood.* Paper submitted for publication.

Duke, N. K., V. S. Bennett-Armistead, and E. M. Roberts. 2002. "Incorporating Informational Text in the Primary Grades." In *Comprehensive Reading Instruction Across the Grade Levels*, edited by C. Roller, 40–54. Newark, DE: International Reading Association.

Duke, N. K., and V. S. Bennett-Armistead, with A. Huxley, M. Johnson, D. McClurkin, E. Roberts, C. Rosen, E. Vogel. (in press). *Using Informational Text in the Primary Grades: Research-Based Practices.* To be published by Scholastic Professional Books.

Duke, N. K., and J. Kays. 1998. "Can I Say 'Once upon a Time'?": Kindergarten Children Developing Knowledge of Information Book Language. *Early Childhood Research Quarterly* 13: 295–318.

Duke, N. K., J. P. Martineau, K. A. Frank, and V. S. Bennett-Armistead. 2002. *3.6 Minutes per Day: What Happens When We Diversify Genres Used in First Grade Classrooms?* [working title]. Manuscript in preparation.

Duthie, C. 1994. "Nonfiction: A Genre Study for the Primary Classroom." *Language Arts* 71: 588–594.

Duthie, C. 1996. *True Stories: Nonfiction in the Primary Classroom*. York, ME: Stenhouse.

Education Department, Western Australia. 1995. *First Steps*. Portsmouth, NH: Heinemann.

Fisher, A. 2001. "Implementing Graphic Organizer Notebooks: The Art and Science of Teaching Content." *The Reading Teacher* 55: 116–120.

Fletcher, R., and J. Portalupi. 2001. *Nonfiction Craft Lessons: Teaching Informational Writing K–8*. York, ME: Stenhouse.

Fountas, I. C., and G. S. Pinnell. 1996. *Guided Reading: Good First Teaching for All Children*. Portsmouth, NH: Heinemann.

Fountas, I. C., and G. S. Pinnell. 2001. *Guided Readers and Writers Grades 3–6: Teaching Comprehension, Genre, and Content Literacy*. Portsmouth, NH: Heinemann.

Forte, I., and S. Schurr. 1996. *Graphic Organizers and Planning Outlines for Authentic Instruction and Assessment*. Nashville, TN: Incentive Publications.

Freedman, A., and P. Medway, eds. 1994. *Genre and the New Rhetoric*. Bristol, PA: Taylor and Francis.

Fry, E., J. Kress, and D. Fountoukidis. 2000. *The Reading Teacher's Book of Lists*. Paramus, NJ: Prentice Hall.

Graves, M., and B. Graves. 1994. *Scaffolding Reading Experiences: Designs for Student Success*. Norwood, MA: Christopher Gordon.

Green, P. 1992. *A Matter of Fact: Using Factual Texts in the Classroom*. Winnipeg, Ontario, Canada: Peguis.

Guillaume, A. 1998. "Learning with Text in the Primary Grades." *Reading Teacher* 51 (3): 476–486.

Guthrie, J. T., P. Van Meter, A. D. McCann, A. Wigfield, L. Bennett, C. C. Poundstone, M. E. Rice, F. M. Faibisch, B. Hunt, and A. M. Mitchell. 1996. "Growth of Literacy Engagement: Changes in Motivations and Strategies During Concept-Oriented Reading Instruction." *Reading Research Quarterly* 31: 306–332.

Harvey, S. 1998. *Nonfiction Matters: Reading, Writing and Research in Grades 3–8*. York, ME: Stenhouse Publishers.

Harvey, S. and A. Goudvis. 2000. *Strategies That Work*. York, ME: Stenhouse Publishers.

Hoff, D. 2002. "U.S. Students Rank Among World's Best and Worst Readers." *Education Week* (January): p2.

Hoyt, L. 1992. "Many Ways of Knowing." *The Reading Teacher* 45 (4): 580–584.

Hoyt, L. 1999. *Revisit, Reflect, Retell: Strategies for Improving Reading Comprehension.* Portsmouth, NH: Heinemann.

Hoyt, L. 2000. *Snapshots: Literacy Minilessons Up Close.* Portsmouth, NH: Heinemann.

Hoyt, L. 2002. *Make It Real: Strategies for Success with Informational Texts.* Portsmouth, NH: Heinemann.

Hyerle, D. 1996. *Visual Tools for Constructing Knowledge.* Alexandria, VA: Association for Supervision and Curriculum Development.

Jobe, R., and M. Dayton-Sakari. 2002. *Info-Kids: How to Use Nonfiction to Turn Reluctant Readers into Enthusiastic Learners.* York, ME: Stenhouse.

Kamil, M. L., and D. M. Lane. 1998. "Researching the Relation Between Technology and Literacy: An Agenda for the 21st Century." In *Literacy for the 21st Century: Technological Transformations in a Post-Typographic World*, edited by D. R. Reinking, L. D. Labbo, M. Mckenna, and R. Kieffer, 235–251. Mahwah, NJ: Lawrence Erlbaum.

Keene, E. O., and S. Zimmerman. 1997. *Mosaic of Thought: Teaching Comprehension in a Reader's Workshop.* Portsmouth, NH: Heinemann.

Mann, C. 2002. "1491." *Atlantic Monthly* 289 (3): 41–53.

Marland, M. 1977. *Language Across the Curriculum.* London, UK: Heinemann.

Mason, J. M., C. L. Peterman, B. M. Powell, and B. M. Kerr. 1989. "Reading and Writing Attempts by Kindergartners After Book Reading by Teachers." In *Reading and Writing Connections*, edited by J. M. Mason, 105–120. Boston: Allyn and Bacon.

Meek, M. 1996. *Information and Book Learning.* Stroud, UK: Thimble Press.

Mohan, B. 2001. "The Second Language as Medium of Learning." In *English as a Second Language in the Mainstream: Teaching, Learning, and Identity*, edited by B. Mohan, C. Leung, and C. Davison. London: Longman.

Moline, S. 1995. *I See What You Mean: Children at Work with Visual Information.* Melbourne, Australia: Longman.

Moline, S. 2001. *Information Tool Kit: Using Nonfiction Genres and Visual Texts (Levels A–C),* Carlsbad, CA: Dominie.

Mooney, M. 1995. *Exploring New Horizons with Guided Reading.* Worthington, OH: SRA Macmillan/McGraw-Hill.

Mooney, M. E. 2001. *Text Forms and Features: A Resource for Intentional Teaching.* Katonah, NY: Richard C. Owen Publishers Inc.

Mooney, M. E. 1990. *Reading To, With, and By Children.* Katonah, NY: Richard C. Owen Publishers Inc.

Ogle, D., and C. L. Z. Blachowicz. 2002. "Beyond Literature Circles, Helping Students Comprehend Informational Texts" In *Comprehension Instruction: Research-Based Best Practices,* edited by Cathy Collins Block and Michael Pressley, pp. 259–274. New York: The Guilford Press.

Opitz, M., and T. Raskinski. 1998. *Good-bye Round Robin: 25 Effective Oral Reading Strategies.* Portsmouth, NH: Heinemann.

Parkes, B. 2000. *Read It Again: Revisiting Shared Reading.* York, ME: Stenhouse Publishers.

Pearson, P. D. 2000. "New Developments in Comprehension Instruction," presented in Madison, WI, June 2000.

Pelligrini, A. D., J. C. Perlmutter, L. Galda, and G. H. Brody. 1990. "Joint Reading Between Black Head Start Children and Their Mothers." *Child Development* 61: 443–453.

Portalupi, J., and R. Fletcher. 2001. *Nonfiction Craft Lessons: Teaching Informational Writing K–8.* Portland, ME: Stenhouse.

Pressley, M. 2000. "What Should Comprehension Instruction Be the Instruction Of?" In *Handbook of Reading Research,* edited by M. L. Kamil, P. B. Mosenthal, P. D. Pearson, and R. Barr. Mahwah, NJ: Erlbaum.

Purcell-Gates, V., and N. K. Duke. 2001, August. *Explicit Explanation/Teaching of Informational Text Genres: A Model for Research.* Paper presented at Crossing Borders: Connecting Science and Literacy conference, a conference sponsored by the National Science Foundation, Baltimore, MD.

Rice, D. 2002. "Using Trade Books in Teaching Elementary Science: Facts and Fallacies." *The Reading Teacher* 55 (3): 552–566.

Routman, R. 2000. *Conversations.* Portsmouth, NH: Heinemann.

Schiefele, U., A. Krapp, and A. Winteler. 1992. "Interest as a Predictor of Academic Achievement: A Meta-Analysis of Research." In *The Role of Interest in Learning and Development,* edited by K. A. Renninger, S. Hidi, and A. Krapp, 183–211. Mahwah, NJ: Lawrence Erlbaum.

Secretary's Commission on Achieving Necessary Skills. 1992. *What Work Requires of Schools: A SCANS report for America 2000.* Washington D.C.: U.S. Department of Labor.

Smith, M. C. 2000. "The Real-World Reading Practices of Adults." *Journal of Literacy Research* 32: 25–32.

Stead, T. 2001. *Is That a Fact? Teaching Nonfiction Writing K–3.* York, ME: Stenhouse Publishers.

Taberski, S. 2000. *On Solid Ground: Strategies for Teaching Reading K–3*. Portsmouth, NH: Heinemann.

Trussell-Cullen, A. 1999. *Starting with the Real World: Strategies for Developing Non-fiction Reading and Writing*, K–8. Carlsbad, CA: Dominie.

Venezky, R. L. 1982. The Origins of the Present Day Chasm Between Adult Literacy Needs and School Literacy Instruction. *Visible Language* 16: pp. 112–127.

Walpole, S. 1999. "Changing Texts, Changing Thinking: Changing Demands of New Science Textbooks." *The Reading Teacher* 52: 357–370.

Wilson, P. T., and R. C. Anderson. 1986. "What They Don't Know Will Hurt Them: The Role of Prior Knowledge in Comprehension." In *Reading Comprehension from Research to Practice*, edited by J. Oransano, 31–48. Mahwah, NJ: Lawrence Erlbaum.

Wormeli, R. 2001. "Writing in the Content Areas." In *Meet Me in the Middle*, York, ME: Stenhouse Publishers.

Index